MANAGING PF

MANAGING PEOPLE

Dipak Kumar Bhattacharyya

EXCEL BOOKS

ISBN : 81-7446-161-2

First Edition: New Delhi, 1999
Reprint: 1999
Reprint: 2000

EXCEL BOOKS
A-45, Naraina, Phase-I
New Delhi-110 028

Printed at
EXCEL PRINTERS
C-206 Naraina, Phase-I,
New Delhi-110 028

ABOUT THE SERIES

Institute of Management Technology (IMT), Ghaziabad is a prestigious management institute, being one of the top ten business schools of India. The institute has recently launched an innovative project on publications. One of the important constituents of this project is production of study material/books for its Distance Learning Programme (DLP). We believe, that whatever mode of learning, print material would continue to be the basic requirement for any educational programme despite revolution in electronic media and other modes of delivery. It has therefore been decided to publish quality material both for core subjects as well as for electives. The material is written in such a manner that it can be used both by student managers studying management courses through conventional mode or distance learning.

It is a painstaking venture to produce such material. However, we have launched this humble project with confidence to meet the long felt need of management education. Quality being a hallmark, we adopted a rigorous procedure for selection of authors, reviewers, production team and publisher. We are glad to present "Managing People" by Dipak Kumar Bhattacharyya.

N.K. UBEROI
Chief Executive
DLP

CONTENTS

DEVELOPMENT AND CONCEPTS OF HRD

LEARNING OBJECTIVES

This chapter focuses on:

☐ history and development of HRD

☐ the differences between Personnel, HRM and HRD

☐ the various concepts and objectives of HRD

☐ the importance of HRD in functioning of organisations

CONTENT OUTLINE

1.1 INTRODUCTION

Ever since the emergence of Personnel or Human Resource Management function, the emphasis was more on legal aspects. The corporate group was entrusted primarily to comply with legal requirements, in the spate of enormous government regulations, which one after another were introduced to protect the rights of workmen.

With the advent of civilisation, social progress and political power, the concept of labour welfare as a separate corporate function has gained ground.

The personnel function moved a long way from statutory labour welfare function to Human Resource Development to cope with the challenges ahead. The changing environment demands more from this profession. Already this function is gaining importance, if not more, atleast at par with the other two vital cores in Industrial army–Production and Marketing.

1.1.1 History

Management of Human Resources, is a subject of relatively recent origin though the concept upon which the theory is based dates back to 400 B.C. (Chaldeans Inventive Wage Plans). Minimum Wage and Incentive Wage Plans were in Babylonian Codes of Hammurabi around 1800 B.C. The Chinese, as early as 1650 B.C., had originated the Principle of 'Division of Labour' (Specialisation). The 'Span of Management' and the related concepts of organisation were well understood by Moses around 1200 B.C. In India, Kautilya observed sound base for Systematic Management of human resources, as early as 4th century B.C.

Prior to Industrial Revolution, the status of labour was extremely low and the human relationships between the employer and the employees were characterised by 'Slavery, Serfdom and the guild system'. 'Slavery' was based on negative incentive system and 'serfdom' was based on positive incentive system. However, both these systems have been replaced with the growth of manufacturing and commercial enterprises by 'Guild System' involving 'Master Craftsmen' (the owner) the 'Journey Man' (the travelling workers) and the 'Apprentice'. 'Guild System' marked the beginning of Human Resource Management with involvement of selection, training and development of workers and emergence of collective bargaining over wages and working conditions.

Industrial Revolution followed the new economic doctrine of 'laissez faire'. Industrial organisations, characterised by 'factory system' (a change from 'cottage system' or home centred production system) deteriorated the employer-employee relationship for unhealthy work environment, long working hours, fatigue, monotony, strain, increased possibility of accidents, etc.

Reviewing the history, it is observed that great thrust had been given to Personnel Management functions by business expansion, labour strategies and higher wage rates during World War I (1917). Many of these activities had been initiated for welfare and paternalism. The great depression of 1920-21 threw many personnel men out of jobs and this created a disillusion for this profession. A number of literatures came up round the world during 1920-22, dealing with different areas of personnel administration and by 1923, it is considered that the profession reached the stage of maturity, as organisations started giving importance to this profession, recognising its imperativeness like other core functions: Production and Marketing.

1.1.2 Development Process

Tracing the history, we find that personnel function was derived from the introduction of welfare and charitable activity. Initially, welfare was percieved as a moral duty and later it was considered as a precondition for industrial efficiency.

The second development sprung from the employers endeavours to cope with the challenges of trade unionism.

The third phase of development could be attributed to the development of the concept of 'Humanisation of Work'.

1.1.2A *Factors which are responsible for development of this profession in a phased manner from world's perspepctive can be listed as follows*

–   Technological changes are taking place at a rapid pace throughout the world. Such changes have a great bearing upon personnel functions because they fundamentally change the relationship between people and work though from an overall point of view they induce a major change in the economic system and the structure of the society.

–   The rising competition both at home and abroad (in case of international trade) virtually reduces the profit to the level of production cost (unless the industry is monopolist). The free movement of technology from one country to another does not allow any production process to monopolise the particular technology of their use.

–   The rise of consumerism, government protection and international competition developed the necessity to maintain quality and price, which completely redress the opportunity to follow the traditional production method.

–   Social changes are also taking place at a fast pace. Business function is no longer mere multiplication of profits. Organisation being a part of the society, also owes towards society.

–   The political development also restructured trade unionism. Trade unionists are no longer a mere wage bargainers.

–   The structural changes in employment (more oriented towards white collared jobs, gradual decline of unskilled jobs) and changes in sectoral distribution of employment (more geared to tertiary or service sectors) also bought a great challenge to the employers.

For personnel profession, all these challenges have a great impact on their functions.

Alienating and dehumanising effect of repetitive and monotonous tasks, in the wake of technological advancements is a universal phenomenon. Effective utilisation of human resources under this technological environment is the prime challenge before today's personnel profession. Even in the United States of America (USA) at present level of production, particularly for workers in the service industries, it is estimated only 50 per cent of the potential is available from existing human skills, initiative and energy. About 12 million employees are now considered obsolete in the USA, which includes a considerable number of engineers and technical people. Manpower obsolescence is also being faced by Japanese industries. Other industrially advanced countries are also facing similar crisis.

The history of evolution and growth of Personnel Management in India is not very old. The Royal Commission on Labour in 1931 for the first time recommended for the abolition of "Jobbers System" and appointment of Labour Officers to deal with the recruitment and to settle their grievances. The Factories Act, 1948, statutorily made it obligatory for the industries to appoint labour welfare officers. Today Personnel Management function in India encompasses all the professional disciplines like welfare, Industrial relations, Personnel administration, Human resource development (HRD), etc.

The general functional areas of Personnel vis-a-vis HRD professionals can be grouped under five major heads as below:

1. Determining and staffing for employment needs,
2. Measuring performance and developing employee potential,
3. Preserving effective employee-management relationships,
4. Uncovering and resolving employee problems,
5. Anticipating and coping with organisational change.

The new changes have extended the functional horizon to many. From a legalistic approach it extended to human relations; from a mere passive factor of production, employees are now perceived as human resources. The functional demand therefore call from many areas like; Management by anticipation, more use of work teams by small group activities/Quality circles, practising Total quality management culture, etc.

1.2 HUMAN RESOURCE DEVELOPMENT AS A SEPARATE PERSONNEL DISCIPLINE

So far, our discussion centres around personnel functions. At this stage we will delineate Human Resource Development (HRD) as a separate discipline of Personnel Management. But before we go into the details of HRD functions, brief understanding of the historical process is considered necessary to appreciate the importance of HRD functions in today's organisation.

It is believed that Kurl Lewin's (1947) studies of behaviour of small groups and setting up of National Training Laboratories are the first steps for HRD profession, which till late in 1940's was the domain of psychiatrists, psychologists, counsellors, nurses and furthered the concept of human relations training and the experiential approach. Participants in training groups (T-groups) effectively identified problems, acquired the skills and also actively collaborated in the problem-solving process. Training group leaders, unshakling their traditional role of instructors, became facilitators and focused on how the individual relates to and interacts with other individuals and with groups and get them trained on leadership and its influence, handling conflict, expressing feeling, giving and receiving feedback, competition and cooperation, problem solving and increasing awareness on oneself and ones impact on others.

In 1969, 'Handbook of Structured Experiences for Human Relations Training ' was published by University Associates giving structured experiences with guidelines for training and development. Subsequent publication of handbooks for groups facilitators in 1972 and 1973 furthered the process of developing training and organisation development vis-a-vis Human Resource Development as a recognised area of professional endeavour, delineating as a new profession, encompassing personnel function.

1.3 HUMAN RESOURCE MANAGEMENT (HRM) AND HUMAN RESOURCE DEVELOPMENT (HRD)

In the introductory submission, we have discussed the development process of HRD delineating it from traditional Personnel Management functions and Human Resource Management. Before we go for defining the concept, definition and objectives of HRD, it is further necessary to study the factors which developed the concept of HRM, replacing the traditional concept of Labour Welfare and Personnel Management. These factors are:

  a. Search for Competitive Advantage: The Competitive Advantage School of Thought (pioneered by Beer, 1985, Trichy, Fombrun and Devenna, 1982) argued that better utilisation of human resources is necessary to achieve competitive advantage by an organisation and by any nation.

  b. Models of Excellence: Study of successful organisations as 'Models of Excellence' by Peters and Waterman (1982) and Kanter (1984) evinced the interest of HRM, as models of excellent companies isolating it from traditional Personnel Management Functions.

  c. Failure of Personnel Management: Management of Human Resources as a mainstream management activity has been advocated by Skinner (1981) and many others as their studies show Personnel Management's failure to promote potential benefits of effective management of people.

  d. Decline in Trade Union Pressure: Changing economic and political climate around the world resulted in decline in trade union pressure on management. This necessitated switch in emphasis from collective issues (traditional Industrial Relations approach) to individual and cooperative issues i.e. the Human Resource Management approach.

  e. Changes in the Workforce and the nature of work: Structural change in the occupational pattern is now a world wide phenomena, of which India is also no exception. Technology, increased requirements of skill and knowledge, occupational shifts, restructuring of production, new quality system requirement, etc. are now demanding better educated new generation of workers, who obviously have higher expectations from their organisations. Such trend calls for redefining employer-employee relationship associated with Human Resource Management.

All these factors listed above revolutionised the concept of traditional personnel management, which is restricted to utilisation of human resources complying with mainly statutes and coping with the challenges of trade unionism and led to the development of HRM as another form of response for sustaining better employer–employee relations.

HRM is a sub-system of the total management system. This is the responsibility of all managers, irrespective of their functions, disciplines and levels. HRM is primarily concerned with the management of people, individuals or groups at work, as also their inter-relationship. HRD, OD and IR are separate aspects of a broader concept of HRM. However, in reality each of these concepts overlap in practice, can not be viewed in isolation. HRM practices, to succeed, must go concurrently with HRD, OD interventions. Sound IR systems can not be visualised without good HRD practices.

1.4 HRM VERSUS PERSONNEL MANAGEMENT

HRM is a distinctive approach and it is possible to distinguish it from traditional Personnel Management in three different ways as follows:

a. The first approach is by simple retitling of Personnel Management, as many companies did by renaming their Personnel Department as HR department.

b. The second approach is by reconceptualising and reorganising personnel roles in line with the conceptual frame work of Harvard Business School (1985), i.e. subsuming personnel and labour relation activities in four policy areas like– employee influence, human resource flow, reward systems and work systems, differentiating HRM from Personnel Management concepts pioneered by Institute of Personnel Management , UK, i.e. employee relations, employee resourcing and employee development. Thus, it is apparent that HRM concept categorises employee relations (industrial relations) as a separate strategic functions, which fall under the traditional Personnel Management function.

c. The third approach designates HRM as a distinctively different and new approach for management. This approach integrates HRM into Strategic Management and emphasises on full utilisation of Human Resources.

At this stage, it is necessary to develop a definition of HRM. Let us define the term Human Resources first. Human Resources is the total knowledge, skills, creative abilities, talents, aptitudes, values, attitudes and beliefs of people of an organisation. There is, however, difference of opinion among many experts as some of them consider human resources are not only the people, who are part of the organisation, i.e. the direct employees, it includes customers (TQM concept) and others who are having variety of other relationships with the organisation. Integrating the concept of human resources with management, we can define HRM as an approach to identify right people for the right job. It also includes the process of socialising such identified people to integrate them with the organisation, train them for increasing their functional skill, develop them for both identified and unidentified future roles, place them in right tasks and roles, motivate them to perform well and inculcate in them a sense of belongingness.

Within the HRM there are two major activities, the first is concerned with the recruitment, selection, placement, compensation and appraisal of the human resources (personnel function), more commonly termed as Human Resource Utilisation (HRU) function. The other group of functions are directed towards working with the existing human resources in order to improve their efficiency and effectiveness. Such activities are also designed to enable the existing members of the organisation to assume new roles and functions. These activities are concerned with Human Resource Development (HRD).

1.5 HRD CONCEPTS

HRD is concerned with an organised series of learning activities, within a specified time limit, designed to produce behavioural change in the learner (Naddler, 1969). From the organisational context, therefore, HRD is a process which helps employees of an organisation to improve their functional capabilities for their present and future roles, to develop their general capabilities, to harness their inner potentialities both for their self and organisational development and to develop organisational culture to sustain harmonious superior-subordinate relationships, teamwork, motivation, quality and a sense of belongingness.

There are a lot of misconceptions about training, education and development functions vis-a-vis HRD. Essentially, HRD activities are designed to make people effective in their present job position, which is a part of training function. But when the focus is on future identifiable job it becomes a part of education function. For future unidentifiable jobs i.e. to develop capabilities for a future position or new activities within the organisation, which are not very specific at the present stage, it becomes a part of development function.

Without precisely knowing the functions of training, education and development, it would further make it difficult for us to appreciate the objectives, roles and significance of HRD in an organisation. In the succeeding paragraphs we will take a cursory view to these functions before we go for elaborating on other issues of HRD.

1.5.1 Training

Training concerns people already employed with the organisation and whose jobs are so defined that we are able to identify what should be the desired job behaviours. The focus on training programmes should be such, so as to enable the individual to perform more effectively in his present job position. Training is needed when a person is hired without the requisite skills, attitude or knowledge or after putting the person on the job, we are able to identify his deficiencies that are possible to rectify through training. Even in cases, where an employee may be performing very well, change in procedures, materials, processes may stimulate the need for further training. Total Quality Management (TQM), Small Group Activities (SGA) or Quality Circles (QC) concepts are now calling for new areas of training for employees to make them functionally more effective in their restructured jobs. We have discussed these issues in a separate supplementary note. For effective results, the responsibility for training should be on the immediate supervisor of the trainee. As the pay-off of training is verifiable on the job, the supervisor is expected to see the results and therefore, he is the right person to allocate physical and financial resources to improve his human resources. However, in most of the organisations supervisors are made responsible for identification of training needs and their role is restricted to impart technical skill enriching training. For conceptual and human skills, training is given by a specialised group of trainers. Training can either be conducted through In-house programmes or by retaining professional trainers/consultants.

The evaluation of training is done in direct relation to the job. At the end of the training, it is expected that there should be some identifiable changes in job behaviour. Where no such changes in job behaviour could be identified, we expect there may be one or more of the following problems: ineffective training programme, lack of linkage between the training programme and the job or negative reinforcements in the work situation. Evaluation of training is easy because of its job relatedness.

1.5.2 Education

Education experiences benefit those who are employed and who are required to be gradually equipped for other positions in the organisation. Thus, education component of HRD is future oriented for identifiable job positions. Since return on investment from education is unclear or unascertainable, very few organisations are prepared to invest on employee education programmes unless future needs or manpower plan of the organisation substantiates the possibility of redeployment of employees after completion of education programme.

Many organisations allow their employees to go on study leave for pursuing institutional studies on areas like, Management, Accounting and Finance, Quality, Engineering or even for Research, which are having relevance to organisational needs. Employees are allowed to draw their pay and get reimbursement of actual cost for study during this period and such leave is not debited against employees' leave account.

Some organisations encourage their employees to get enrolled in part time evening programmes and allow them reimbursement of actual cost. In India a number of institutes are encouraging sponsored candidates to pursue studies as full time students.

However, education within the organisation is considered as a better alternative as it simultaneously ensures employee on-the-job activities and learning of new techniques for their future roles. For example, some organisations with their in-house talents run professional programmes for their employees like, Engineering Degree Courses of Institute of Engineers, Indian Institute of Metals, Management Degree Courses of All India Management Association, National Institute of Personnel Management., ICFAI Business School, International Institute of Management Science, etc. This is considered more cost effective than the earlier two methods and this also reduces the time-lag between the time of education experience and its application on the new job.

Employee education calls for attitudinal changes of corporate leaders as they should be prepared at the outset to invest in the future of individuals who may or may not remain with the organisation. It is also necessary to identify individuals who are future-oriented. Evaluation of employee education is difficult when there is considerable time-lag between learning and its actual on-the-job application.

1.5.3 Development

Development component of HRD is to conduct learning experiences for a future undefined job. The focus being on future undefined job an organisation before going ahead with employee development, must be able to identify individuals who enjoy high risk and new undefined challenging jobs. Such risk takers may not necessarily confine in higher levels of an organisation, even though conventionally, development function rests in the higher levels only. Since decisions on investment in employee development are taken at higher levels and people at higher levels are considered to be more knowledgeable (both by virtue of experience and educational background) than people at lower levels, hardly few organisations consider it right for risking the investment to develop employees at lower level. However, experience shows, carefully planned development experiences can be helpful in realising the human potentials, irrespective of their hierarchical levels and functional areas.

Before the introduction of computers in Indian organisations, computer literacy was considered as a development function. At present, however, TQM, Business Process Re-engineering, Bench Marking, ISO:9000 Quality Systems, Value Engineering, etc. are considered as new areas of development.

Valuation of employee development programmes is extremely difficult both in terms of return on investment and application of learned experiences, for obvious time-lag, in the organisation.

However, success of training, i.e. HRD efforts of an organisation in the form of education and development programmes, largely depends on simultaneous changes in the organisation, which is known as Organisational Development (OD). Changes in the employees behaviour (for training, education and development programmes) is reinforced by changes in the organisation by OD process, which uses many strategies and interventions. Hence, HRD efforts should be in congruencewith OD interventions.

1.6 OBJECTIVES OF HRD

From the foregoing discussion, objectives of HRD can be listed as follows:

1. To develop capabilities of all individuals working in an organisation in relation to their present role.
2. To develop capabilities of all such individuals in relation to their future role.
3. To develop better inter-personal and employer-employee relationships in an organisation.
4. To develop team spirit.
5. To develop coordination among different units of an organisation.
6. To develop organisational health by continuous renewal of individual capabilities (averting manpower obsolescence) keeping pace with the technological changes.

Objectives of HRD can be made clear when we highlight the importance of human resources in line with the examination process of the 'Baldridge Award', which is given at an international level to a quality organisation. Objectives of HRD practices in an organisation should be to put efforts to develop/and realise the full potential of the workforce, including management and to maintain an environment conducive to total participation, quality leadership and personal and organisational growth. In an organisation there are six units (foci's) which are concerned with HRD namely person, role, dyad, team, interteam and organisation. The effectiveness of one contributes in turn to the effectiveness of the others.

HRD objectives can also be couched in line with W. Edward Deming's fourteen principles for quality improvement in an organisation. Here we won't discuss the fourteen principles but we will focus on only those points which are related to HRD objectives These are:

1. Institute training on the job.
2. Breakdown barriers between departments to build teamwork.

3.   Drive fear out of the work place.

4.   Create conditions to enable employees to take pride in their workmanship.

5.   Institute programme of education and self improvement.

At this stage for better appreciation, we will review the HRD objectives of two leading companies in India.

EXHIBIT 1

HRD OBJECTIVES OF SIEMENS LIMITED

•   Development of employees is the primary task of the company.

•   It is the policy of Siemens to recruit, train, develop and advance employees within the company.

To achieve these objectives Siemens have laid down their policies as under:

•   Recruitment of quality manpower and their retention.

•   Recruitment mainly at entry level.

•   Plan and monitor career development staff to perform effectively in their present jobs; groom potential managers for higher responsibilities.

•   To introduce and sustain an objective system of evaluation of performance based on result.

•   Performance as the sole criterion for increments and promotion.

•   Use of training as the strategic factor for competitive advantage.

•   To nurture a spirit of entrepreneurship among employees.

•   Work in close collaboration with Corporate Human Resources of Siemens AG.

•   Timely and correct communication for fostering the spirit of openness.

•   To ensure transparency in decision making.

   -   Self-motivated employees

   -   Employee Commitment

   -   Commitment of results.

EXHIBIT 2

W.S. INDUSTRIES INDIA LIMITED

•   To plan and induct appropriate manpower in terms of knowledge, skill and attitude.

•   To provide opportunities for growth to employee in terms of remuneration, career and skill endowment.

- To practice equity and fairness in all its dealings with employees.
- To continuously enhance knowledge, skill of employees for the performance of their present and future task through education and training.
- To create an organisational climate to have a highly motivated work force.
- To prepare employees for easy and faster adaptation to change.

1.7 ROLE AND SIGNIFICANCE OF HRD

For any dynamic and growth oriented organisation to survive in a fast changing environment, HRD activities play a very curcial role. Recent economic restructuring in India at macro level influenced the need for production at unit (micro) level and production restructuring necessitated labour restructuring vis-a-vis restructuring of HRD activities at organisations. Training and retraining and redeployment has now become buzz word in corporate circle as market globalisation (which is an outcome of economic restructuring programme), delicensing and freeflow of technology (as per New Industrial Policy of July, 1991) intensified competition, rendering traditional skills and knowledge redundant. Many organisations in India are now threatened with manpower obsolescence to withstand which, HRD activities have now received prime importance.

Increased morale and motivation of employees no doubt are necessarry to achieve productivity and functional effectiveness. But these alone cannot sustain a dynamic organisation, unless effort and competencies of human resources are renewed constantly, developing and enabling organisational culture. An enabling organisation culture is possible when employees of an organisation are found to use their initiative, take risks, experiment, innovate and make things happen.

Hence, role and significance of HRD in an organisation can be appreciated when we consider the fast changing environment coupled with technological change and intensified competition. This has necessitated the need for renewal of capablities of people working in the organisation which are simultaneously reinforced by changes in the organisation by Organisational Developmental (OD) process.

The role and significance of HRD can further be appreciated when we consider different sub-systems of HRD like, Performance Appraisal, Career Planning and Development, Manpower Planning, Management Succession and Development, Training (which includes the role of education and development discussed earlier), Organisational Development (OD), Quality of Work Life (QWL), etc. Discussions in all such sub-systems have been made separately in Chapter II of the book.

REVIEW QUESTIONS

1. Briefly discuss the history of development of HRD function? Or Discuss the process of development of HRD suitably delineating it from Labour Welfare and Personnel Management?

2. What are the general functional areas of HRD? Answer these keeping in view the HRD functions of any organisation?

3. Do you think HRM and HRD are different functions? How the concept of HRD developed in an organisation?

4. Differentiate between training, education and development? Discuss how they are related to HRD?

5. What are the objectives of HRD function? Briefly explain the HRD objectives of any leading organisation?

6. Explain the role and significance of HRD. Do you think, in the present context in India, we really need HRD professionals in our organisations?

7. Short Notes:

    a. Guild System

    b. Structural change in employment

    c. Kurl Lewin

    d. T– Groups

    e. Competitive Advantage

    f. Human Resource Utilisation (HRU)

2 MANAGEMENT OF HRD UNIT

LEARNING OBJECTIVES

This chapter aims at discussing:

☐ the structure of HRD unit in an organisation

☐ the role of HRD manager and consultants in increasing workers' productivity and organisations profitability

CONTENT OUTLINE

2.1 INTRODUCTION

In the foregoing chapter we have discussed different sub-systems of HRD. In this chapter we will consider the functioning of integrated HRD systems in an organisation. It is pertinent to mention Indian organisations, by and large, have Personnel functions integrated with HRD functions, excepting a few who have separate HRD department, exclusively for HRD functions. Most of the organisations, therefore, merely retitled the designation of their personnel core by either calling Human Resource Manager or Human Resource Development Manager. Yet there are some organisations, who have isolated their HRD as training function, entrusting the responsibility to Management Development Officers or Principals of their Management Development Centres. Public sector giants like Steel Authority of India Limited (SAIL), Indian Oil Corporation (IOC), NTPC, ONGC, Coal India, have set up their own Management Development Institutions/Centres. Departmental undertakings like Indian Ordinance Factories, Indian Railways also have their separate management development centres. Many commercial banks, Reserve Bank of India, Regional Rural Banks, financial institutions like Industrial Development Bank of India (IDBI), Industrial Finance Corporation of India (IFCI), Industrial Credit and Investment Corporation of India (ICICI), insurance companies like, Life Insurance Corporation of India, General Insurance Corporation of India, have set up their own staff training colleges for developing their human resources. Similarly private companies like, TISCO, Kirloskar Group, Reliance, Lakshmi Group, Hinduja Group, Modern Group, Lalbhai Group have their own management development centres to develop and train their human resources.

We have shown three different organisational charts for Personnel/Human Resources/ HRD function for a large company, for a company where personnel/HRD functions are integrated and for an organisation where HRD is shown as a separate department. But before we review the organisation charts, it is important to discuss the principles pertaining to focus, structure and functioning, which we should consider while designing an integrated HRD organisation.

2.1.1 Focus of the HRD System

Reviewing the definition, role, significance, purpose and objectives of HRD as explained in the foregoing chapters, it is evident that HRD department of an organisation focuses on the following important areas:

1. *Increasing the 'enabling' capabilities* by developing human resources, organisational health, team spirit and increasing employment motivation and productivity.

2. *Focus on balanced organisational culture* by conducting period surveys, workshops, discussions stimulating openness, mutual trust, team spirit, creativity, initiative, mutuality, collaboration, delegation, autonomy, respect, management of mistakes, management of conflict, etc.

3. *Focus on learning contextual factors* from different professional bodies like NIPM, ISTD, HRD Network, etc. These professional bodies, through their publications, seminars and workshops, share the experiences of the corporate world.

4. *Focus on periodic reviewing of HRD system* which may call for redesigning

Performance Appraisal, Job-rotation, Reward System, Career Planning, Promotion, Selection, Induction, Training and Development Programme, etc.

5. *Focus on integrating HRD* with other corporate functions like Production, Marketing, Finance, Material, Corporate Planning, etc. Such integration will strengthen the development of 'enabling' organisation.

6. *Focus on diffusion of HRD function* involving line managers in various HRD aspects like Training of subordinates, Performance Appraisal, Promotion, Placement, Selection, Career Planning, etc. Line people by virtue of their rich experience may effectively contribute to these HRD areas. Moreover, their active association will accentuate the process of developing an integrated HRD system in an organisation.

7. *Focus on working with unions* by taking them into confidence and collaborating with them. That unions can also play a positive role in furthering the organisation is evident from number of examples like, Syndicate Bank Employees Union very recently collaborated with the management to reduce the Non-performing Assets (i.e. bad debt realisation).

2.2 STRUCTURE OF HRD SYSTEM

The precise organisational plan for an HRD Department depends on the type of organisation in which it is located and the size of organisation. Here we are giving hypothetical examples of organisation structure for three different organisations to appreciate the functioning of HRD departments in different organisations.

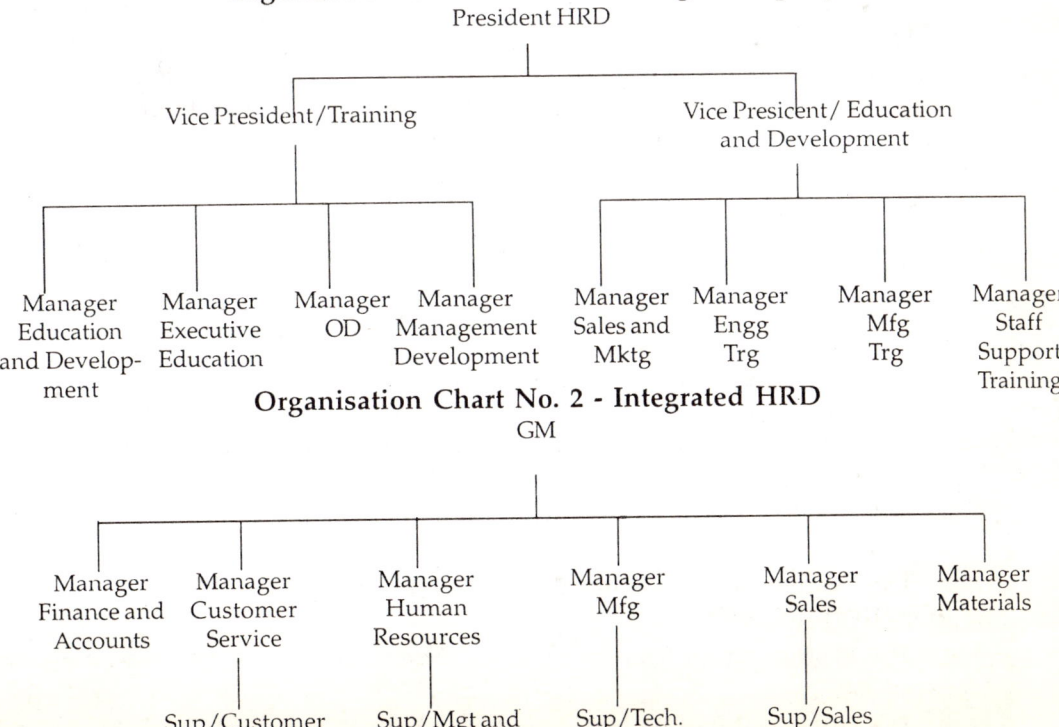

Organisation Chart No. 1 for a Large Company
President HRD

Vice President/Training — Vice President/ Education and Development

Manager Education and Development | Manager Executive Education | Manager OD | Manager Management Development | Manager Sales and Mktg | Manager Engg Trg | Manager Mfg Trg | Manager Staff Support Training

Organisation Chart No. 2 - Integrated HRD
GM

Manager Finance and Accounts | Manager Customer Service | Manager Human Resources | Manager Mfg | Manager Sales | Manager Materials

Sup/Customer Service Trg | Sup/Mgt and Clerical Trg | Sup/Tech. Trg | Sup/Sales Trg

Organisation Chart No. 3 - HRD as a Separate Department

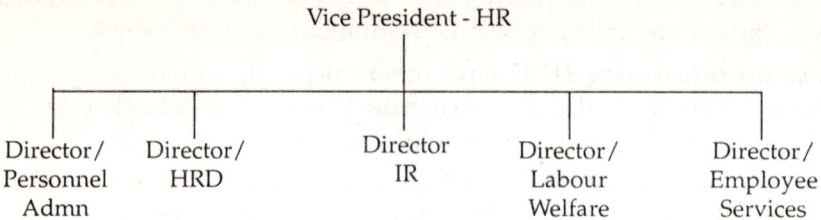

Vice President - HR

| Director/ Personnel Admn | Director/ HRD | Director IR | Director/ Labour Welfare | Director/ Employee Services |

Structure of HRD system organisations was briefly discussed in the introductory part of this chapter, duly illustrating an integrated HRD structure and HRD as a separate functional identity in an organisation. Here we will discuss the basic principles while structuring HRD Department of an organisation.

Needless to mention that the structure of HRD Department differs from organisation to organisation, for difference in size, nature of activity, philosophy and attitude. However, following principles are usually followed in every organisation, while it goes for structuring HRD Department.

1. Developing an identity of HRD which may or may not encompass other personnel functions.

2. Establishing credibility for the HRD function, which is possible by entrusting the reponsibility for HRD at a higher level in an organisational hierarchy.

3. Balancing integration and differentiation. Differentiation can be ensured by not diluting the HRD function with traditional personnel management and industrial relations function, which is possible by entrusting the functional responsibilities to different departmental heads as illustrated in the organisation Chart No. 3 Similarly, integration can be achieved by diffusion of HRD function with other major corporate functions like; Marketing, Production (as explained earlier) and line functions, as inputs from these areas can enrich the functioning of HRD department, structure of which has been illustrated in Organisation Chart No.2.

4. Likewise, while structuring an HRD department of an organisation it should be ensured that it has linkages with external systems and internal systems, i.e. HRD department should represent various task groups, ad hoc committees, etc.

5. Finally, structure of HRD department should be developed so that it can sustain a monitoring mechanism.

Basic principles governing the functioning of HRD system in an organisation has been made amply clear by ASTD, while describing different roles of HRD Manager. However, basic essence of functioning principles of HRD systems can be listed as follows:

a. HRD system should develop a strong feed-back and re-enforcing mechanism.

b. The system should balance qualitative (subjective) and quantitative (objective) decisions.

c. The system should balance the requirement of internal and external expertise.

d. The system should be introduced in a phased manner.

2.3 ROLE OF HRD MANAGER

From the foregoing discussions, it is apparent that the primary goal of HRD is to increase worker's productivity and firm's profitability as investment in HRD improves workers' skill and enhance motivation. The other goal of HRD is to prevent obsolescence at all levels. To achieve these two goals, HRD Manager of any organisation plays following two important roles:

> 1. To assist people in obtaining the knowledge and skills they need for present and future jobs and to assist them in attaining their personal goals.

> 2. To play the 'enabling' role, providing the right context in which human performance occurs and the organisation reaches its stated objectives.

American Society for Training and Development (ASTD, 1988) identified eleven roles of HRD Manager, which can be enumerated as follows:

> 1. *Administrator:* The role of providing coordination and support services for the delivery of HRD programmes and services.

> 2. *Evaluator:* The role of identifying the impact of an intervention on individual or organisational effectiveness.

> 3. *Individual Career Development Advisor:* The role of helping individuals to assess personal competencies, values and goals and to identify, plan and implement development and career actions.

> 4. *HRD Manager:* The role of supporting and leading a group's work and linking that work with total organisation.

> 5. *Instructor/Facilitator:* The role of presenting information, directing structured learning experiences and managing group discussions and group process.

> 6. *Marketer:* The role of marketing and contracting for HRD viewpoints, programmes and services.

> 7. *Material Developer:* The role of producing written and/or electronically mediated instructional materials.

> 8. *Needs Analyst:* The role of identifying ideal and actual performance and performance conditions and determining causes of discrepancies.

> 9. *Organisational Change:* The role of influencing and supporting changes in organisational behaviour.

> 10. *Programme Designer:* The role of preparing objectives, defining content and selecting and sequencing activities for a specific intervention.

> 11. *Researcher:* The role of identifying, developing or testing new information (theory, concepts, technology, models, hardware) and translating these two implications for improved individual or organisational performance.

R. Wayne Pace, Philip C. Smith and Gordon Mills (1991) after reviewing the eleven roles of HRD, as indicated by ASTD, grouped all these roles into four major areas, as below:

A.   Analytic

> a. Needs Analyst

    b.   Researcher

    c.   Evaluator

B. Developmental

    a.   Programme Designer

    b.   Materials Developer

C. Instrumental

    a.   Instructor/Facilitator

    b.   Organisation Change Agent

    c.   Marketer

D. Mediational

    a.   HRD Manager

    b.   Individual Career Development Advisor

    c.   Administrator

2.4 ROLE OF CONSULTANTS IN HRD

In HRD, consultants play a very crucial role, particularly in following areas:

a. In designing a career plan for the employees, many organisations prefer to retain the services of consultant. Career planning is a very complicated function of the organisation as faulty career planning may ultimately lead to dissatisfaction of the employees, who may leave the present organisation to get employed elsewhere. Many Indian organisations are facing the crisis of mid-career shift for not adopting the suitable career plan for their employees. SAIL, the public sector giant very recently lost 400 of their key and middle level executives to join newly formed private steel manufacturing companies. The chairman of SAIL in a recent press briefing lamented such large scale exodus of steel executives from SAIL will cost heavy for the organisation, as in developing an executive with exposure in steel requires 10 to 15 years time. All such executives who have left SAIL attributed reasons which inter alia include absence of better career progression and more financial benefits in private steel manufacturing companies. Banks and other financial institutions are also facing similar unpleasant situation for recent liberalisation of financial market vis-a-vis emergence of private banks/ foreign banks/ global financial institutions, etc. Very recently State Bank of India retained the services of world famous management consultant, McKinsey for restructuring the organisation, which inter alia includes developing suitable career plans for their employees.

b. Manpower Planning has also become a crucial function for HRD consultants especially in the wake of increasing manpower obsolescence for technological changes in Indian industries.

c. Similarly in Training and Development, Performance Appraisal, Recruitment, Selection and Placement, developing suitable promotional policies, Management Succession and Management Development, etc., HRD consultants are playing a very crucial role.

Before engaging HRD consultants, it is necessarry to consider following important points:

(i) When an organisation needs to expand its capabilites on 'Crash Basis'. Under these circumstances the organisation cannot afford to rely solely on untried competence of this internal resource alone. It needs to hire the services of consultants, who are having the required expertise.

(ii) Similarly an organisation may require to avail the services of specialised experts in some areas, where it does not have the requisite internal skill and knowledge. This is particularly relevant in cases like training and management development programmes where we find many organisations retaining the consultants to impart training on TQM, ISO:9000, Quality Circles, Value Engineering, Business Process Re-engineering, Bench Marketing, Just in-Time, Total Productive Maintenance, etc.

(iii) HRD consultants are also engaged in cases where objectivity or corporate strategy leverage to a job done needs to be given.

Whatever may be reasons for retaining the services of HRD consultans, we find their increasing use in corporate sector for efficient result, cost benefit, less time-lag, etc.

REVIEW QUESTIONS

1. What should be your focus areas for designing an effective HRD system? Which focus would you consider more important than others?

2. What important factors should be considered while structuring HRD unit of an organisation? Illustrate your answer with an organisation chart of HRD department of any organisation.

3. Briefly discuss the principles for functioning of HRD system of an organisation. What are the important roles of HRD Manager?

4. Do you think for an organisation it is necessary to retain an HRD consultant? What are the possible advantages and disadvantages in retaining HRD Consultants?

5. Short Notes:

    1. Integrated HRD Functions
    2. Enabling Organisation
    3. Analytic Role
    4. Instrumental Role

3 MANPOWER AND CAREER PLANNING AND DEVELOPMENT

LEARNING OBJECTIVES

This chapter discusses:

☐ activities required for manpower planning

☐ job anaylsis, job description and job specification

☐ the various techniques applied for manpower planning

☐ importance and advantages of career development

☐ the process involved in career planning

☐ the perceptive changes made in career planning to enable employees to keep pace with the changing requirements

CONTENT OUTLINE

3.1 INTRODUCTION

To achieve HRD objectives, HRD system may include number of process mechanisms or sub-systems as explained in the earlier chapter. For students' convenience we have discussed these mechanisms grouping them in two different clusters considering the functional proximity. In this chapter we will discuss Manpower planning and Career planning and development.

3.2 MANPOWER PLANNING

Manpower is a primary resource without which other resources, physical and financial, cannot be put into use. Even a fully automatic unit requires manpower to run it and also to plan for further improvement.

Manpower planning is a process by which an organisation can move from its current manpower position to its desired manpower position. Through manpower planning an organisation strives to have the right number and the right kind of people at the right places at the right time. However, the above definition focuses only the assessment of manpower needs in an organisation. More appropriately manpower may be defined as a strategy for acquisition, utilisation, improvement and retention of human resources.

3.2.1 Activities required for Manpower Planning

Manpower planning consists of a series of activites, which can be listed as follows:

a. Forecasting future manpower requirements: This is done either in terms of mathematical projections or in terms of judgemental estimates. Mathematical projections are done extrapolating factors like economic environment, developing trends in industry, etc. Judgemental estimates on the other hand are done depending on the specific future plans of a company.

b. Preparing an inventory of present manpower: Such inventory contains data about each employee's skills, abilities, work preferences and other items of information. Inventory of manpower resources helps in assessing the extent of deploying such resources optimally.

c. Anticipating problems of manpower: This can be done by projecting present resources into the future and comparing the same with the forecast of manpower requirements. This helps in determining the quantitative and qualitative adequacy of manpower.

d. Meeting manpower requirements: This can be achieved through planning recruitment and selection, training and development, induction and placement, promotion and transfer, motivation and compensation, to ensure that future manpower requirements are correctly met.

3.3 STEPS FOR MANPOWER PLANNING

Manpower planning precedes a number of steps. Such steps can be briefly discussed as follows.

A. Job Analysis

To start with job analysis is done to differentiate one job from the other. Job is defined as collection or aggregation of tasks, duties and responsibilities which are assigned to an individual employee. Job analysis, therefore, provides requisite information about a job. It is a process of determining the nature of a specific job through a detailed and systematic study. Job analysis provides the following information:

a. *Job identification* which is done by providing a title or a code number for each job.

b. *Job characteristics*, location, physical setting, hazards and discomforts of a job.

c. *Job assignment*, specific operations and tasks which make an assignment, its importance, simplicity, complexity and the responsibility.

d. *Materials*, tools and equipment required for a job.

e. *Job performance*, nature of operation, (lifting, handling, drilling, setting up, etc.)

f. *Personal attributes* like experience, training, physical strength, mental capabilities, aptitudes, other skills, etc. required for efficient performance of the job.

g. *Job relationship*, scope for advancement, patterns for promotions, direction or leadership form, etc.

Sources of Information

The sources from which information is obtained are as follows:

a. From the workers or employees who are performing the job.

b. From those who are supervising the job, e.g., supervisors and foreman.

c. From professional job analysts (consultants), who may be retained to study a job.

Purpose of Job Analysis

Apart from manpower planning, job anlaysis serve the following important purposes of Human Resource Management vis-a-vis development.

a. Recruitment and selection

b. Wages and salary administration

c. Job re-engineering

d. Industrial engineering activity

e. Employees training and management development

f. Performance Appraisal

g. Health and safety

B. Job Description and Job Specification

After the Job analysis process is over, job description and job specification are developed before going into the successive steps of manpower planning. Job descriptions are recording of duties, responsibilities and conditions needed for satisfactory performance of a particular job. Both the terms job description and job specification are interchangeably used. However, it is appropriate to distinguish the term description to cover job content (conditions, tasks and responsibilities) and specification to denote job requirements(i.e. qualities necessarry in the worker for satisfactory performance of the job).

Thus, job specifications translate job description into human qualifications required for successful performance of a job.

C.   Developing Work Rules

Most of the organisations, after developing job description and job specifications, develop work rules, which are some pre-determined decisions about certain course of action that may be taken when certain contingencies arise. Organisations develop such work rules in a documented form and use the same as a control device to ensure predictability of behaviour. Starting and stopping of work/rest periods, time keeping, in-subordination, fighting or drinking on the job, smoking, report of injuries, etc. are normally incorporated in such work rules.

D. Application of Industrial Engineering Techniques

Work Study, Method Study and Work Measurement Techniques are also applied as a preceding step for manpower planning. These techniques provide opportunity for effective use of plant and equipment, effective use of human effort, measurement of human work, better ways of doing things, developing predetermined standard times, etc.

E. Other Factors

a. *Layout:* Layout of a factory influences determination of manpower requirement. Some plant and equipment work in isolation (like Lathe, Drilling machine) while some other work in group continously (like Excavators, Group Drive System). When a group of machines work in union, the whole group may be attended by one or more persons. But when machines are not in continuous operation, a single person may look after more than one equipment. Thus, requirement of manpower may vary for the layout and machine arrangement in a shopfloor or factory.

b. *Statutory requirements:* For certain positions in mines, electrical installations, hazardous places (chemical plant, etc.), welfare amenities need to be provided as per statutory regulations. Positions like Welfare officers, Safety officers, Medical officers fall under this category.

c. *Shifts:* Number of manpower required also depend on whether the work would be carried out in general shift or in shifts. Number of working shifts will decide the requirement of manpower.

d. *Leave reserve:* Since no one can work all the days for one reason or the other, certain allowances need to be given while working out manpower requirement. Apart from unpredictable absence, workers are allowed leave systematically for a specific period in a year. Conventionally, 20 per cent. allowance for weekly off and leave reserves are allowed in factories while working out manpower requirements. In mines, however, rate of absenteeism being high, such allowance percentage is on much higher side.

3.4 OBJECTIVES OF MANPOWER PLANNING

The first objective of manpower planning is to integrate planning and control of manpower resources with the organisational planning to ensure best possible utilisation of all resources.

The next objective is to coordinate manpower policies of the organisation. Recruitment and selection, training and development programmes, placement and induction programmes, promotion and transfer policies, decisions on remuneration and rewards, etc. affect the future needs of manpower. Without proper coordination of manpower policies with each such decision, it is difficult to achieve the corporate objectives. Therefore, it is necessary to harmonise such objectives (corporate) with manpower planning system. Without coordination, company's plans may get frustrated for not having the right people at the right place and time. Subsequent objectives of manpower planning are:

    a.   To achieve efficiency of work in all spheres of corporate body,

    b.   To ensure cost minimisation and

    c.   To eliminate all types of wastages including waste of time.

3.4.1 Manpower Demand Forecasting

Manpower Demand Forecasting is influenced by primarily two important factors, volume of output and the level of productivity. Manpower requirement may change due to output volume or mix, which calls for analysis of performance.

Similarly as the level of productivity alters over time, it also affects manpower requirements. This calls for analysis of productivity.

3.4.2 Analysis of Performance

To derive the manpower demand, it is necessary to estimate the manpower requirements in relation to the work load. To start with, each unit of manpower (more conveniently defined as man-hours or man-days) required for different categories of job to accomplish the job in its entirety is determined. After such determination the total work load are related to manpower units of different categories and then finally the total requirement of manpower of different categories is determined. Such analysis, therefore, calls for analysis of performance either through direct or indirect methods.

Direct analysis is to review past performance to derive a ratio between two variables (workload and manpower category). This can be done either by relating to a particular point of time or by averaging figure over a period of time.

Indirect analysis is based on the estimates made on past experience. Thus, it is less systematic than Direct analysis. However, for short range forecasts, indirect analysis is more preferred, as experienced managers can make this analysis after putting considerable thought.

For making both direct and indirect analysis, interdependence among different factors needs to be considered.

3.4.3 Analysis of Productivity

Productivity has two major components – technological change and manpower utilisation. As technological change requires huge capital investment, organisations look for better manpower utilisation to achieve increased productivity. With better human relations, productivity can be increased. Again the rates of productivity vary substantially with the level of performance. Manpower demand forecasting can be made more effective once we consider both the variables, i.e. the performance and productivity. Most of the public sector enterprises are over staffed, presumably for inadequate emphasis on both these two aspects simultaneously.

3.5 USE OF MATHEMATICAL MODELS FOR MANPOWER FORECASTING

For short-range forecasts usually normal budgetary process is followed. Human resource budgets and projections are generally based on estimates of workload. Conversion ratios that translate workload data into personnel demand estimates may be used for a short-range demand forecast. For example, as sales increase by a certain percentage, a manufacturing concern may determine that the number of employees in certain departments or divisions must also increase. The use of conversion ratios provides only a rough approximation of the number of employees required and may indicate very little about the types of personnel needed. Job analysis information is helpful in this respect because it defines the educational, experience and skill requirements of future employees.

Long-range human resource forecasting is more amenable to mathematical and statistical models. Mathematical models used in human resource forecasting are based on selected key variables that affect the organisation's overall human resource needs. Some mathematical models contain both internal and external variables. Following mathematical models, developed by Elmer H. Burack and Rober D. Smith (1977), incorporates a number of factors for forecasting overall employment in an organisation:

$$E_n = \frac{(L_{agg} + G)\,\frac{1}{x}}{y}$$

Where,

E_n is the estimated level of personnel demand in 'n' planning periods (e.g. five years).

L_{agg} is the overall or aggregate level of current business activity in Rupees.

G is the total growth in business activity anticipated from today through period 'n' in today's Rupees.

X is the average productivity improvement anticipated from today through planning period 'n'.

Y is the conversion figure relating today's activity to the human resources required (total level of today's business activity divided by the current number of personnel). It reflects the level of business activity per person.

The major purpose of this model is to predict E_n, the level of human resources necessary in 'n' periods. Prior to plugging numbers into the model, estimates of G, X and Y must be made.

Illustration:

Assume that we currently have Rs 10,00,000 of sales (L_{agg}) in today's Rupees. Further assume that by 2000 our sales will increase by Rs 5,00,000 in today's Rupees (G, rupees adjusted for inflation), that there will be no increase in productivity ($X = 1.0$) and that each of today's employees can support Rs 50,000/- worth of sales (Y). Substituting these values into the formula we obtain:

$$E_{2000} = \frac{(10,00,000 + 5,00,0000)\ \frac{1}{1.0}}{50,000}$$

= 30 Sales Persons

3.6 CAREER PLANNING AND DEVELOPMENT

Career Planning and Development essentially means process of increasing an employee's potential for advancement and career change. In other words it is a process of planning a series of possible jobs which an individual may hold in an organisation over time and developing strategies designed to provide necessarry job skills as the opportunity arises. Therefore, career development relates to the readiness for progression through a series of positions during an individual's working life. Career Development may be differentiated from Career Planning and Career Management. Career Development is the systematic process of guiding the movement of human resources of an enterprise through the different hierarchical positions whereas career planning is a process of establishing career objectives of an employee (or by the person himself) and developing planning strategies to achieve them including activities which help in making choices with respect to occupations, organisation's job assignment and self development measures. Career management, on the other hand, relates to specific human resource management activities, such as recruitment, selection, placement and appraisal to facilitate career development.

3.6.1 Why Career Development

Every organisation needs to provide career development opportunities to its employees. Indian corporate sector at present is facing major restructuring to keep pace with the economic restructuring programme of the country. Market globalisation, technology upgradation, import liberalisation, delicensing, increased competition, together have now prompted Indian companies to restructure their production vis-a-vis organisation. Redeploying the manpower through proper training in restructured jobs is one of the important priorities for the organisations, particularly for those who are at down the level. But employees with matching skill and knowledge now find them in better bargaining position for increased job mobility. Most of the foreign and multinational companies are now winning away the employees with matching skill knowledge from Indian organisations with better offer for pay and career. Therefore, poor career development programme may affect an organisation at least in two ways:

a. High employee turnover, particularly those who are in the beginning of their career.

b. Decreasing employment involvement.

Recruitment expenses, training expenses and reduced performance during orientation (loss of output, increased wastages, etc.) together add to the cost of employee turnover.

Decreased employee involvement also affects functional efficiency and productivity of the employees. Other important reasons for career development can be listed as follows:

a. Changing environment is now making jobs more complex. Suitable career development programmes enable employees to be better prepared for future positions in the organisation. It also gets the opportunity to identify prospective managers from within. Manning vacancies from within is cost efficient and at the same time the system motivates the employees.

b. Suitable career development programmes enable the organisations to receive maximum contribution from employees. Since this helps the employees to enhance their skills for higher positions, both under-utilisation of employees potential work energy and their under-employment can be avoided.

c. Career development makes employees more adaptable to changing requirements of the organisations. Requirements of the organisation may change due to new technology. Computer Numerically Controlled Technology (CNC), Numerically Controlled Technology (NC), Direct Numerically Controlled Technology (DNC) and Flexible Manufacturing System (FMS) or new management philosophy and style, like Just-in-time Manufacturing, Total Quality Management, etc.

d. It provides an objective basis to describe the steps of progression in a given organisation and therefore, minimises unfair promotion by discretion. Thus, suitable career development programme avoids employees resentment on promotion issues which has now become a major causal factor of industrial disputes in India.

e. Most of the organisations are now also manned by women and other minority classes of the employees. Career development programme ensures equitable opportunity for career progression of these classes of employees also. Thus, it meets the requirements for equal employment opportunities for all.

f. Career development programme gives opportunities to employees to acquire more skills, obtain desired jobs, share increased responsibility, enjoy scope of job mobility and derive increased job satisfaction.

3.7 SIGNIFICANCE, PURPOSE AND TYPES OF CAREER DEVELOPMENT PROGRAMMES:

3.7.1 Significance and advantages of Career Development

The significance and advantages of career development both from organisation's and employees' point of view can be summed up as follows:

1. It reduces employee turnover by providing increased promotional avenues.

2. It improves employee morale and motivation.

3. It enables organisations to man promotional vacancies internally, thereby, provides opportunities to reduce the cost of managerial recruitment.

4. It ensures better utilisation of employees' skills and provides increased work satisfaction to employees.

5. It makes employees adaptable to the changing requirement of the organisation.

6. It reduces industrial disputes related to promotional matters and thereby provides opportunity to the organisations to sustain harmonious industrial relations.

7. Employees' loyalty and committment to the organisation can be substantially increased and thereby organisations can enjoy the privilege of increased employee productivity.

8. Career Development Programme being an objective description of career progression, it ensures equitable promotional decisions even for women and minorities in an organisation.

3.7.2 Purposes and Objectives of Career Development

The purposes and objectives of Career Development Programme can be listed as below:

1. To attract and retain effective persons in an organisation.

2. To utilise human resources optimally.

3. To improve morale and motivation level of employees.

4. To reduce employee turnover.

5. To practise a balanced 'promotion from within' policy.

6. To make employees adaptable to changes.

7. To increase employees' loyalty and committment to the organisations.

8. To maintain harmonious industrial relations.

9. To inculcate equitable employment practices providing equal career progression opportunities to women and minorities.

3.7.3 Types of Career Development Programmes

In an organisation, there are different types of development programmes to enrich different skills of human resources. These include organisation development, employee development, management development and career development. Organisational Developmental Programmes are planned and managed from the top to bring about planned organisational changes for increasing the organisational effectiveness. Management Development is concerned with upgrading the manager's skills, knowledge and abilities. Employee development programmes intend to enhance the ability of the employees to enable them to accomplish additional job responsibilities. Career Development, on the other hand, is a process of guiding the movement of human resources through different hierarchical levels.

Whatever may be the differences, career development is interelated with other human resource development functions.

3.8 STEPS IN CAREER PLANNING PROCESS

Career Planning Process involves different activities or steps in an organisation. Such steps are listed below:

Step I. Preparing Personal Skill Inventories.

The first step is to prepare personnel skills inventories. Such skills inventories is an information system which contains data on employees skills and career goals. In addition, such data bank provides following information:

a. The organisations structure and the persons manning different positions in the organisations. Their age, education, experience, training and career goals, status, duties and responsibilities.

b. The performance records and ratings, inter-personal abilities of the employees.

c. Their preferred location, desires and constraints.

d. Whether the present strength is short or surplus to the requirements. If it is short, the extent of shortage at different levels and the organisational resources available to make good such shortages in future. If it is surplus, the measures available to redeploy them through proper restructuring.

e. Future requirement of manpower for expansion or diversification of the company or for natural wastages like death, disability, retirement, discharge and dismissal, resignation, etc.

In most of the organisations, such information are computerised and periodically reviewed and updated. After preparation of personnel skills inventories and additional data, it is necessary to develop career paths for employees.

Step II. Developing Career Paths

Career paths are logical mapping of jobs, which represent a potential progression track that an employee may follow over time. Such mapping of job progressions are done in the form of career ladders clubbing together similar lines of occupations in job families. Job families are groups of homogeneous jobs, i.e. jobs with similar characteristics.

Step III. Put the right man at the right place

The third step in career planning process is to identify suitable employees who have the ability, potentiality and willingness to take up higher responsibilities and rise up to the organisational ladder. For this, most of the organisations have performance appraisal and merit rating system. This system enables organisations to compare the performance measures of different individuals in terms of job requirement and help in identifying training requirements for instance, selecting for promotions, providing financial rewards etc.

Step IV. Impart Training

The next step in career planning process is formulation and implementation of Training and Development programmes. Such programmes should be designed in a manner that can improve technical and conceptual skills of employees, particularly in those areas which have been identified as deficient through performance appraisal system. For continuous change in environment it is also necessary to constantly renew and update the knowledge and skills of the employees to make them adaptable to the changing requirements. Most of the Indian organisations today impart training to their employees to make them adaptable to the changing requirements. Most of the Indian organisations today impart training to their employees on Quality Circles (Small Group Activities), Value Engineering Techniques, Total Quality Management Principles, ISO:9000, etc.

Step V. Review and counsel

In addition to the above, career planning process is also concerned with developing suitable promotions and transfer policies, periodic review of career development plans and career counselling. Career counselling provides guidance to the employees on occupational training, education and career goals.

3.9 FUTURE OF CAREER PLANNING AND DEVELOPMENT IN INDIA - SOME ORGANISATIONAL ISSUES

In India we do not have any empirical studies worth the name on Career Planning and Development. New challenges like competition, market globalisation, deregulation and total quality management have now made it imperative for organisations to restructure their career planning and development programmes to retain best talents. Companies like Bajaj Auto, Arvind Mills, Gujarat Ambuja, Essar Gujarat, Reliance Industries, Bombay Dyeing, Hindustan Lever, Crompton Greaves, Tatas, etc., have now brought in many perceptive changes in career planning for their employees to keep pace with the changing requirements. Such perceptive changes can be listed as below:

a. Most of the companies now consider employees as their important assets. The concept of total quality management considers every employee as customer (internal) to the organisation. Making employees entrepreneurs for the organisation and empowering them is now compelling the organisation to redesign career progression tracks to attract and retain the best employees. Making people psychologicaly prepared for ownership, some organisations are also experimenting with flatter organisation structure with adequate decentralisation.

b. For manning senior executive positions organisations are now giving more importance to knowledge than functional skills. This perhaps is the only reason for selecting people even in their early thirties for senior managerial posts.

c. Organisations are now more keen to get rid of those employees who are now redundant due to changing requirements by offering golden handshake, rather than developing these persons for better redeployment.

d. Merit is now getting overriding priority than seniority. This, therefore, renders career progression paths less important. Many, however, feel that even with greater priority of merit over seniority, career progression paths do not become completely meaningless, since for even promotion by merit, the lines of progression paths are relevant. For any succession planning or promotion planning this is still important.

In addition, organisational restructuring programmes are now rendering many employees surplus and it has become a major problem for the organisations to redeploy employees in restructured jobs. Career plan has now become a global issue. Most of the organisations, fearing employee turnover are now working on redesigning jobs which can offer employees recognition, creativity (bilateral transfers, etc.), challenges and empowerments.

REVIEW QUESTIONS

1. What is Career Development? Why is it important for an organisation? Does it differ from Career Planning?

2. Do you think career planning should be individual centred or organisation centred? Briefly discuss the career planning programme of an organisation you know.

3. What are the factors you consider important for successful career planning?

4. Discuss the important steps in career planning process?

5. What is the future of career planning and career development in India? Do you think recent economic restructuring has any bearing with such process? Elaborate your answer.

6. Define Manpower Planning. What are the activities involved in manpower planning?

7. What is Optimum Manpower Planning? You have been retained by an organisation to develop manpower planning system, what factors would you recommend them to consider for effective manpower planning?

8. What is Job analysis? In what way is job analysis important for manpower planning? In what other areas of Human Resources Management, job analysis is important?

9. What is Manpower Demand Forecasting? What factors would you consider for manpower demand forecasting?

10. Short Notes:
    1. Career plateauing
    2. Career ladders
    3. Job families
    4. Skill inventories
    5. Judgemental estimate of manpower
    6. Job description
    7. Work rules
    8. Industrial engineering techniques
    9. Leave reserve
    10. Indirect analysis of manpower

CHAPTER

4 RECRUITMENT, SELECTION, INDUCTION AND PLACEMENT

LEARNING OBJECTIVES

This chapter aims at discussing:

☐ the definition, function and process of recruitment

☐ the process and framing of a selection procedure

☐ different types of interviews

☐ the organisation's and employees point of view on what a good induction programme should be

☐ the various steps involved in induction programme

☐ the importance of induction and placement activities

CONTENT OUTLINE

4.1 INTRODUCTION

Recruitmnt, selection, induction and placement are important tools for procuring and effectively using human resources in an organisation while recruitment involves employing suitably trained work force, selection helps in choosing the right candidate for the right job. Induction and Placement is putting the men to the right jobs. This chapter focuses on these four important organisational activities.

4.2 RECRUITMENT

Personnel Management functions in recent years have assumed importance for its increasing emphasis on human resources. Traditional approach to personnel management was to ensure routine human resource maintenance functions for the organisations. But recently, radical changes in human resources management, i.e. perceiving human resources like other important resources (physical and financial) of an organisation has developed new areas for personnel management. The human resources are the people who are part of the organisation. Broadly, they may be direct employees, the customers served, part-time persons, temporary employees or consultants or any person or persons with a variety of other relationships to the organisation. Within the human resources area, there are two major activities. The first is concerned with the recruitment, selection, placement, compensation and appraisal of the human resources (these are known as Human Resources Utilisation Functions or Personnel Functions). The other functions are directed to work with the existing human resources, improving their efficiency and effectiveness. These are known as Human Resources Development (HRD) functions which are designed to enable existing human resources to learn activities for their effective functioning in the present jobs, future identifiable jobs and so also for future undefined jobs.

For increasing importance of human resources, it is now imperative for all organisations to retain the manpower and at the same time to recruit and select best possible talents in the country. Most of the organisations are now facing technological changes, resulting radical change in the recruitment process. Such a technological change, inter alia, calls for hiring manpower having higher skills and knowledge, which were not so far available. However, when we consider the recruitment of manpower for unskilled jobs, there seem to be no apparent problems for the organisation, as these people are abundantly available in our country for obvious high rate of unemployment. For high technology employees, i.e. mostly those who are in managerial positions with professional skills, recruitment function is more complex and dynamic.

4.2.1 Definition

The term recruitment may be defined as the process to discover sources of man-power to meet the requirements or the staffing schedule and to employ effective measures for attracting that manpower in adequate number to facilitate the selection of an efficient working force.

4.2.2 Functions

The first important task of recruitment functions is to frame a recruitment policy. Framing a recruitment policy calls for review of manpower requirement. i.e. it should be adequately supported by an effective manpower forecasting . Manpower planning and so also manpower forecasting of an organisation depends on many important factors like present nature of work, possible change in the future working of the organisation, the manpower records and information available in the organisation for the present strength, the diversification plans and programmes of the organisation, the environmental change and the change necessary in the organisation to respond to such environmental change, etc. Most of the organisations, in principle, believe in recruiting best possible manpower from outside the organisation. However, recruitment policy of some organisations consider recruiting the employees based on the recommendation of the present employees or recruiting employees from the wards of the existing employees.

For example, in Tata organisation, there is a system to recruit employees for unskilled jobs, both technical and non-technical nature, from the wards of the existing employees. Such a policy of recruitment in Tata organisation has been accepted in principle and Tata, in their manufacturing units, maintain a separate employment exchange records to enlist the names and other details of the employees, wards to offer them employment as and when vacancy arises. But such type of recruitment policy is not followed while hiring manpower for managerial jobs. In such cases, companies are looking for best available talents. Thus, they go either for advertising the vacancies in leading newspapers of the country, even in good professional journals or they may go in for recruitment of such managerial manpower by effecting campus interview, in different technical and professional institutions. At times, some companies are also going for retaining the services of recruitment consultants. Such recruitment consultants, having maintained a separate data bank for the prospective job seekers, can make available list of prospective managerial manpower to such companies. In addition to the framing of recruitment policy, each organisation for making their recruitment a scientific process of selection, carry out regular forecasting of manpower recruitments.

4.2.3 Internal Recruitment

In some cases, organisations are also trying to internally man higher managerial vacancies from their existing employees. In those cases, organisations need to develop their existing manpower adopting suitable training and development functions. Training and development may not necessarily always ensure availability of the best talents internally. Organisations are then compelled to recruit from outside sources, mentioned above.

4.2.4 Recruitment policy

Sound recruitment policy calls for adopting scientific process of recruitment, i.e. those techniques, which are modern and scientific. Recruitment policy also requires to consider the high cost of managerial turnover. Unless a company adopts a suitable recruitment policy, it may not be possible for the company to select right candidate for the right job. A sound recruitment policy, therefore, needs to:

1. Identify, at the outset, the recruitment needs of the organisation
2. Identify the preferred sources of recruitment
3. Frame suitable criteria for selection and finally
4. Consider the cost of recruitment.

4.3 RECRUITMENT PROCESS

As has already been discussed, a particular organisation may effect recruitment either from the internal sources, i.e. by promoting the existing employees for higher positions, or they may go for outside sources. Thus internal and external sources of recruitment can either be resorted to by any organisation, subject to the convenience and feasibility. Recruitment is an art of attracting applicants, from whom the most suitable ones may be selected in a particular job or jobs. Internal recruitment may often avoid the unpleasantness, but it is not necessarily effective because it does not allow the organisation to get many alternatives to select the best available. The external sources being open, it gives opportunity to an organisation to tap the best or suitable candidates from widely dispersed areas. The requisition for recruitment contains brief description of the post, qualification and experience required, etc. Such requisitions are normally signed by the head of the Personnel Department. External sources of recruitment are taken recourse to keeping in view the type of personnel required. The workmen may be recruited at the gate itself or from the employment exchange. Management trainees are taken from the institutes and universities, effecting campus interview. Senior executives are attracted through advertisements in leading newspapers and magazines. The major sources of recruitment for different types of personnel, therefore, are as follows:

1. Employment exchanges,
2. Consultants and private employment agencies,
3. Advertisements in periodicals and newspapers, radio and TV,
4. Deputation,
5. Universities and Management Institutes,
6. From the source of existing employees,
7. Trade Unions, etc.

The employment exchanges maintain register of candidates seeking various types of jobs. Under Compulsory Notification of Vacancies Act, 1955, the employers are required to notify certain types of vacancies to the nearest employment exchange and recruit candidates from among the applicants registered with them. The skilled and unskilled workers and the clerical staff are mostly recruited through employment exchanges. Private consultants and agencies assist organisations in locating technical and managerial staff. They charge prescribed fees for their services to the organisation.

Advertising in newspapers and magazines, radio and TVs, have now become most effective sources for attracting the prospective candidates. It also helps in building the image for the organisation because through such advertisements, the organisation makes available certain information, like their product, their market share, their turn-over value, etc. to the public in general and target consumers in particular. Since written press insertions or verbal advertisements through audio and audio-visual methods give the first hand information to the prospective job-seekers, each organisation is required to give as much factual information as possible regarding the job–expectations from the candidates, their age-group, qualifications and experience, salary and perks attached to the positions and important conditions of service, the time-limit and mode of applying, etc. There are some agencies who help organisations in drafting, publishing and broadcasting advertisements.

Deputationists are mainly appointed in public sector undertakings. The civil servants are often deputed for many senior and mid-level positions for a specified time.

Recruitment from universities and management institutes are effected through campus interview. Almost all good private organisations select their management trainees through such method. Some organisations even sponsor the cost of prospective students during their learning to join them after completion of the course.

From the source of existing employees also, recruitment is done by many private organisations to ensure commitment and loyalty and at the same time to motivate the employees. Such type of recruitment, however is restricted only to the clerical and unskilled jobs in most of the cases.

Trade unions also recommend candidates for clerical and unskilled jobs. This practice is not in vogue in many organisations. Only in technical training scheme, trade unions were found to influence the organisations to induct their recommended candidates as apprentices.

4.4 SELECTION

Selection process is different from recruitments. Selection is the assessment of the candidates and finally to choose right candidates from many for the job. Selection, therefore, means rejection of candidates for a position and it is a negative process from this point of view. When there are many candidates, the organisation often short lists candidates in a proportion of number of vacancies, say 1:10 or 1:8, etc. Like recruitment policy, each organisation frames a selection policy to screen the best available talents from many.

4.5 SELECTION PROCESS

Like recruitment, selection process includes both activities relating to internal movement of manpower and external hiring. Each organisation through adequate job analysis and job description, identifies the possible attributes required for different levels and the selection process enables an organisation to match the qualities of the applicants with such attributes. Thus, the first task of selection process is to define the organisation's needs for different positions and so also to assess the available people to determine the best to fill the vcancy. There are different strategic concerns for a selection process.

The first such concern is to develop in an organisation a wide selection and promotion system that supports the overall manpower policy of the organisation.

The second concern is to create internal flow of people to suit the future requirements of the organisation.

The final strategic concern is matching key executives to the organisation's policy.

The process of selection, therefore, starts with the consideration whether internal candidates are available to man the vacancies. Internal selection is now being considered as the best policy to sustain morale of the present employees and the organisation also can reap the motivational benefits by adopting an effective 'promotion from within' policy. Since internal staffing is not always feasible for reasons explained earlier, organisations are often compelled to look at external sources some organisations, to make their selection process scientific, use the internal candidates as their standards to select from outsiders. This selection process is resorted to in those cases where organisations go for both internal recruitment and external hiring.

Developing a structured application form to elicit information from the prospective job seekers is another essential part of selection process. Such structured application form is developed by the organisation in line with the personnel records which are maintained for human resource planning (including the preparation of skill inventories and redeployment programmes).

The selection method, therefore, provides the scientific basis of choosing the best talent from available job-seekers, adopting the above norms. What should be the right selection process depends on the perspective in human resources of different organisations. Thus, there cannot be an universally acceptable selection process for each and every organisation. Despite such differences, any selection process essentially involves the following steps:

1. Preliminary screening of applicants,
2. Review of Application Blanks,
3. Checking references,
4. Physical examination,
5. Psychological testing,
6. Employment interview and
7. Evaluation of the programme.

4.5.1 Framing a Selection Procedure

Framing a selection procedure is important to ensure scientific selection of employees for all levels in an organisation. To match the requirements of the jobs with the attributes of the candidates, the first step is to make a detailed analysis of job content to develop job descriptions. Such job descriptions clearly specify the necessary attributes needed for each job. Most of the organisations, in order to develop a standard job description for each job, determine the level of competencies by adopting industrial engineering techniques like, time study, method study, work measurement, etc.

The next step in selection procedure is to personify such attributes in candidates,. i.e. developing a specification of persons, to define the background education, training, personality and characteristics of the candidates to suit the vacancy position. This in reality is an exericise to pre-portray an ideal candidate for a job.

4.5.2 Preliminary screening of applicants

Number of applications normally received against any advertised vacancy are usually more. This creates the problem of selecting the right persons from many. Moreover, conducting tests and interviews for all the candidates may not be always feasible and at the same time cost efficient. To obviate such problems, most of the organisations sort our unsuitable candidates before going ahead with the selection process. There are many different ways to do such preliminary screening. Some organisations conduct a short tests for all the applications, while best method may be the checking of 'Application Blank'. Each organisation before going for the selection process develops their own standards or potential attributes for the prospective candidates. This helps them also to define the rejection standards. For example for the post of a Stenographer, a particular organisation may define their rejection standards as below.

1. Those who are having a shorthand speed below 100 words per minute and types speed below 40 words per minute.

2. Those who are not having any working experience;

3. Those who are above 35 years age.

By checking 'Application Blank' of the candidates, and organisation may reject a good number of applicants based on the above rejection prarameters. All the above processes, therefore, enable the organisation to short-list the candidates before going ahead with the subsequent stages of selection. The rejection standards, like the ones stated above, may also be mentioned in the advertisement itself so that the number of applicants is minimised.

Some organisations also adopt 'successive-hurdles' technique as an effective screening process. This technique calls for arranging all selection factors in order of importance. For example, if for a particular post aptitude test is considered most important, the first step should be to test the aptitude of the candidates, then the other successive tests, like qualification, job experience, personality etc. may be conducted provided the candidates qualify these hurdles one by one.

4.5.3 Review of Application Blanks

The application blanks form is designed to have detailed information about the applicants. Some organisations have their own printed application blank, while others ask the candidates to give their particulars in a standard format to elicit information like:

a. Personal Data and Biographical Information, i.e., name, address, telephone number, age, sex, marital status, children, nationality, education (school, college, university attended, degree/diploma passed, year of passing, subjects, grade or division obtained etc.), professional qualification and membership of professional bodies, language known (ability to read, write and speak), etc.

b. Chronological employment history for all jobs (with joining and leaving dates in each case of employment change), employer's name, address and nature of business positions held and duties, reason for leaving (if any).

c. Personal circumstances, when available, prepared to serve any where or not.

d. Medical history, brief details of any serious illness, number of days absented during last few years (in case the applicant served earlier some where) on medical grounds, record of hospitalisation (if any), disability, major operation, etc.

e. Interest, hobbies, sports and other activities.

f. Anything else which the applicant may like to add in support of his candidature.

Several other items may be included in the application blank on the specific requirements of the organisation and the job.

Weighted application blanks are also prepared by some organisations to record personal history items associated with the job success. For each item of the application blank, weight factors are pre-determined. Importance of weight factors for different job also vary. For example, for unskilled labourers job, education may be given less weight, while for executive positions, education receives higher weightage. Application blank, therefore, helps in comparing the applicants.

4.5.4 Reference Checking

Some organisations ask for references from the applicants in application blank itself to get information on candidate's character and antecendents. Such references are preferred from earlier employers and schools/colleges/universities who have some acquaintance with the candidates. Organisations try to verify candidates' antecedents from the referencers either over phone, through correspondence or through personal visits. Most of the organisations send a brief questionnaire to such references alongwith a confidential note, requesting them to furnish such details.

4.5.5 Physical Examinations

Physical examinations are also sometimes conducted to assess individual's health status matching them with the physical and environmental conditions of job requirements. For some positions in an organisation physical strain and psychological stress are relatively more. Organisations through job analysis, identify such physical parameters and demand for those from candidates for specific jobs.

4.5.6 Psychological Testing

Generally, psychological testing is used for purposes like, determining training needs and evaluation of training programmes, selection and placement, transfer and promotion, counselling. However, such testing is primarily used for selection and placement. Such tests are of different types like, group or individual tests, instrumental tests, aptitude or achievement tests, personality and interest tests, etc. Group Tests are designed to test a group of candidates simultaneously . Individual tests are for individual candidates at a particular point of time. Instrumental tests can be group tests or individual tests. When it is an individual test, it makes use of different tools to study individual candidate's familiarity and skills. But in case of its application for a group, it involves written test or paper-pencil test to study the written responses of the candidates. Aptitude tests are intended to assess the potentiaility of the applicants to learn the job, while achievement tests enable us to assess how effectively an individual can perform his job. Conventionally, aptitude tests are administered on freshers, i.e. those who are not having any past job experience, while achievement tests are intended for experienced candidates, which are having bearing with job performance. For marketing job and managerial and executive positions such tests have much relevance. However, psychological tests are mostly designed to measure the aptitude and skills of successful job performers. For selection and placement, most of the organisations retain the services of consultants and experts on psychological testing. This minimises the chance of errror in selecting the wrong candidates for different job positions.

4.5.7 Interview

In the literal sense of the word, an interview means a conversation with a purpose. Such purposes are classified under three categories– obtaining information from the candidates, giving information to the candidates and finally to motivate the candidates. The first purpose is intended to get information from candidates regarding their background, experience, education, training and interests to evaluate their suitability as per the requirements of the organisation. The second purpose is to provide the candidates information regarding the organisation, its philosophy, personnel policies, etc. The third purpose is to establish a positive relationship to motivate the prospective candidates to join the organisation. However, all these purposes being successive stages of interview, the subsequent stages will be followed only when the interviewers are prima facie satisfied with the candidates in the first stage.

Personnel department of most of the organisations conducts preliminary interview for the candidates. However, for subsequent interview, a committee of executives is formed to select the right candidates. For managerial and executive positions, organisations prefer to retain the services of consultancy organisations with subject-experts on the selection committee.

There are different types of interviews as under:

a. *The Patterned interview:* This is also known as structured or standardised interview. It is intended to assess the candidate's emotional strength and stability, industry, ability to get along well with others, self-reliance, willingness to accept responsibility, motivation, etc.

b. *Indirect or non-directive interview:* This type of interview is meant for helping the candidates to feel relaxed and free to talk. Interviewers become listeners and allow the candidates to reveal their personality, indepth knowledge in a free and relaxed atmosphere.

c. *Direct Planned interview:* It is a simple question-answer session to ascertain the suitability of the candidates.

d. *Stress interview:* This interview assesses the candidates emotional balance under a situation of tension and stress. Such tension is, therefore, deliberately created by interruptions, provocations, silence, criticism or even by firing questions. Interviewers in such a situation deliberately become more unfriendly and even, at time, hostile. For selection of executives, who are required to work under stress, such method is often adopted.

e. *Group interview:* This method is intended to assess the leadership ability of the candidates. Generally, a topic is given to the candidates to discuss among themselves. The interviewers remain in the background to assess the best leaders, their initiative, poise, adaptability, awareness, inter-personal skills, etc.

f. *Panel or Board interview:* Several interviewers collectively interview a candidate to rate his/her attributes. Generally, such a panel consists of several experts and each of them interview a candidate only in those areas on which they have the requisite expertise.

For conducting a successful interview, interviewers should be adequately competent and trained. Interview should be conducted in a suitable place, it should be well-planned, job descriptions and information about the applicants should be adequately studied, interviewers should be free from any conceivable prejudice, interviewees should be allowed to feel relaxed, beginning and ending of an interview should be made in a best possible friendly manner, etc.

The limitations of traditional selection process like failure to select the right persons for the right jobs, too much emphasis on written tests and interview, result psychometric method which have now been developed by the Indian Institute of Psychometry, Calcutta. This method enables us to quantify the attributes, adding which we can select the candidates in order of their merit. Many organisations today are making use of this method to ensure proper selection of their employees.

4.6 INDUCTION

After selection of employees, the first step is to orient them to organisational life. Induction or orientation programme of an organisation is a process to guide and counsel the employees to familiarise them with the job and the organisation. This process helps an organisation to clarify the terms and conditions of employment, specific job requirements and also to inculcate confidence in the minds of the new entrants.

4.6.1 Objectives

General objectives of such a programme normally are:

1. To introduce new employees with the organisational environment, exposing them to the mission, history and traditions of the organisation, its achievements and future challenges, its personnel policy and expectations from the new employees.

2. To create a positive attitude in the minds of the new employees.

3. To create proper awareness in the new employees enabling them to understand the business of the organisation.

4. To provide opportunity to interact with other fellow employees and also with other managerial employees of the organisation.

A good induction programme should contain following areas which are conveniently distributed under organisation's point of view and employee's point of view.

4.6.1A *Organisation's point of view*

1. History, mission, objectives and philosophy of the organisation.

2. Its product, production process, operations involved, state of technology.

3. Its past achievements, present status and future growth plan.

4. Structure of the organisation and the functions of different departments.

5. Delegation of authority and decision making process.

6. Personnel policies, other miscellaneous policies, practices and regulations.

7. Job descriptions and responsibilities.

8. Expectations from new employees.

4.6.1B *Employee's point of view*

1. Job responsibilities.
2. Office procedures.
3. Grievance handling procedures.
4. Salary and perks.
5. Service rules governing hours of work, overtime, safety, holidays and vacations, absenteeism, pollution control.
6. Rules covering probation, confirmation, promotion opportunities, transfer, etc.
7. Retirement and superannuation benefits.
8. Employee services and welfare activities.
9. Employee's participation in small group activities, suggestion schemes.
10. Performance evaluation.

4.7 STEPS IN INDUCTION PROGRAMME

An induction programme essentially involves following steps:

1. *General orientation:* It includes guided tours in different departments of an organisation, introduction with fellow employees, supervisors and executives, information about the organisations's mission, philosophy, achievements and future plans, etc. Some organisations have their printed manuals, which they give to their new employees to orient them with their induction training programmes for a week or so. The purpose of such general orientation programme is to build a sense of pride in the minds of the new employees and also to create an interest in them about the organisation.

2. *Specific orientation:* This is intended to help new employees to get acclimatised with their new work environment. The supervisor or the departmental boss of the employee takes him on round to his place of work and impart vocational guidance for his particular nature of work. He is also told about the technology, environment and other facilities available in the organisation, prevailing practices and customs and specific expectations from an employee. For executives and managerial employees, targets and key result areas for each of them are given to make them aware of what organisation expects from them.

3. *Follow-up orientation:* This orientation is conducted after some time of initial induction of an employee, i.e. preferably within a period of six months or so. The purpose of such orientation is to give guidance and counsel to the employees to ensure that they are reasonably satisfied and gradually settling with the organisation.

4.8 PLACEMENT

After initial programme is over, an employee is put to a specific job, for which he has been selected. Most of the organisations put new employees on probation for a specified period after which they are confirmed or made permanent, provided they match the organisational requirements. Personnel department periodically reviews the progress of such employees getting feedbacks on their performance from their controlling authority. Some organisations have also a system to extend probationary period, if the employees fail to match to the organisational expectations. Such second placement is known as 'differential placement'.

Placement is defined as assigning employees jobs for which they have been identified as suitable based on the selection techniques. But such definition would be meaningless, if a particular employee is recruited against a particular vacancy. Generally, the question of placement arises when a group of trainees are recruited. Organisations, to identify the true potentiality of an employee in such cases, make provision for short-term placement, during which phase, employees are allowed to work on different jobs, through a systematic job rotation programme. However, at a later stage, permanent placement is effected matching the employees' competence, knowledge, skill and job interest. Other forms of placement have been discussed in the chapter on Transfer and Promotion.

4.9 IMPORTANCE OF INDUCTION AND PLACEMENT

Common use of high technology, increased level of knowledge and skills of the new job entrants, production restructuring and flexibility coupled with perceptive change about human resource, which is now considered as most important resource of an organisation, have now transformed labour as an item for competitive sale and purchase. However, despite the problem of unemployment in India, there still exists dearth of knowledge and skilled workers and so also executives and managers. Recent economic liberalisation programme of the Government of India has now paved the way for entry of multinationals and foreign companies. Market globalisation has further intensified the competition. Development of Total Quality Management philosophy, inter alia, is also demanding sea change in product and service-mix of an organisation. All these together have now increased the scope for job-mobility for employees with knowledge and skills of appropriate type and degree.

Unfortunately, retaining employees after the recruitment and selection is an utterly neglected area in Indian corporate sector. Many organisations spend several lakhs of rupees in terms of job advertisement, conducting tests and interviews, hiring the services of consultants and psychologists etc., for selecting a managerial employee. Weak induction programme, without adequate emphasis on building confidence and sense of belongingness in the minds of the new employees, result in quick separation, so also wastage of colossal sum of money for the organisation. Such experience is quite common in public sector units. Very recently a leading Tata organisation has lost few hundreds of their young engineers and professionals, who left en masse to join elsewhere.

Some organisations, on the contrary, do not review the progress of the new employees, who get permanent automatically after completion of their probationary tenure, despite the reason that they are unproductive.

Thus, a good induction and placement programme needs to ensure employees' retention by keeping their motivation high, while at the same time, getting rid of the unproductive employees within the organisations.

REVIEW QUESTIONS

1. Define Recruitment. What are the important recruitment functions? Why such functions are important for an organisation?

2. What is internal recruitment? Why is it important for an organisation? Do you think it is necessary to have a Recruitment Policy for an organisation?

3. What are the different recruitment processes? Briefly state their merits and demerits.

4. Briefly discuss the importance of selection process and mention the steps involved in such process.

5. You have been retained by an organisation to select few management trainees. What process you think you should consider and why?

6. What is the objective of an Induction Programme? What important areas need to be considered for an effective induction programme?

7. What are the different steps involved in an induction programme? In what way induction and placement have now become important for Indian Organisations?

8. Write Short Notes on:
   a. Differential placement
   b. Job rotation
   c. Probationary period
   d. Follow-up orientation
   e. Stress interview
   f. Application blank
   g. Deputation
   h. Successive hurdles

Application Blank Format

Name of the Post

Advertisement No.

PERSONAL DATA

Full Name: Ms/Mr	Applicant's photograh
Date of birth, State, Marital Status	
Nationally, Whether SC/ST	
Height: ------------cm. Weight: ------------kgs.	Vision: Normal/Corrected Spectacle Lens Nos:
Address to which we should write: Telephone No.	Permanent Address Telephone No.
Father's/Husband's Name and Occupation:	
If you have any relative employed in/or on the Board of our company, please give details.	
Details of previous employment in this company or its sister concerns, with reasons for leaving.	
Details of previous employment elsewhere, with reasons for leaving.	

Languages: Mother tongue	Speak	Read	Write

Education

Examinations	School/ College/ University/ Institute	Years attended		Major subjects	Class, % of marks and ranks
		From	To		

Scholastic Achievements

TRAINING

Name of the Firm/Institution	Period		Details of Training	Stipend, if any
	From	To		

WORK EXPERIENCE

Employer	Period		Position held and nature of work	Salary p.m. Basic Total
	From	To		

EXTRA CURRICULAR ACTIVITIES

Types of activities	At School	At College	Elsewhere
Official position held: Sports Participation Positions held – Captain, Secretary/Manager			

GENERAL INFORMATION

Have you ever been convicted? It so, give full details.

Have you had any major illness, operations or accidents?

Any other information that you would like to furnish:

Name and addresses of three persons other than relatives to whom we may write for references:

Name	Address

Minimum Salary expected:

What is the earliest date you could join, if selected?

We appreciate your time and effort your have spent in completing this application. Would you please check your application to ensure that you have completely and accurately answered each and every question?

I declare that the particulars given above, are to the best of my knowledge, correct and complete and undertake to advise the company immediately of changes, if any, in respect of my particulars given above. I confirm that there is no legal bar in my applying for and accepting the aforementioned employment.

Date	Signature of the applicant

I have verified the certificates and testimonials where necessary.

Date	Officer-in-Charge

TRAINING AND DEVELOPMENT

LEARNING OBJECTIVES

This chapter aims at introducing:

- ☐ the need for manpower training and classification of training programmes on the basis of functional level and occupational categories of employees
- ☐ training for top and middle management
- ☐ Identification of training needs and steps for designing a training programme
- ☐ methods used for training of employees
- ☐ off-the-job methods of training
- ☐ importance, functions and objectives of Performance Appraisal
- ☐ traditional and modern methods of performance appraisal
- ☐ phases of performance counselling.

CONTENT OUTLINE

5.1 INTRODUCTION

In chapter I we have already discussed the need for training and development while defining the objectives, role and significance of HRD in an organisation. In this chapter we will discuss these two issues as important HRD sub-systems.

5.1.1 Definition and Purposes

Training may be defined as systematised tailor made programme to suit the needs of a particular organisation for developing certain attitudes, actions, skills and abililities in employees irrespctive of their functional levels. Training, therefore, serves following important purposes for an organisation:

a. To increase the performance level of an employee and to develop him/her in such a mananer that he/she can rise to the position of higher responsibility.

b. To constantly develop manpower to meet the current as well as future needs of the organisation.

c. To ensure effective utilisation of human resources.

d. To integrate individual goals with the organisational goals creating a climate so that an individual employee can best achieve his goals by attending the goals of the organisation. To be more specific this is the stage of identifying employees with the organisation.

5.1.2 Need for Manpower Training

Most of the organisations prefer internal manning of positions than external hiring for obvious motivational benefits and cost effectiveness. Even though training, prima-facie, emphasises on increasing the performance level of an employee, a continuous training function enables the organisation to develop employees for future responsible positions in the organisation itself.

The needs for manpower training in an organisation may be categorised as follows:

a. *Updating knowledge:* Technological advancement, business environmental changes and new management philosophies have now made it imperative for the organisation to renew and update the knowledge and skill of the employees so that they do not become redundant for obvious functional incompetence. The first and foremost need for manpower training, therefore, is to renew and update knowledge and skills of employees to sustain their effective performance and also to develop them for future managerial positions.

b. *Avoiding obsolescence:* Recent economic liberalisation programmes of Government of India are neccesitating organisational restructuring, which inter alia, calls for training the employees, irrespective of their functional level, for their redeployment in restructured jobs. Therefore, the second important need for training is to avert functional obsolescence.

c. *Improving performance:* Continuous training being required to renew and update knowledge and skills of employees, it makes them functionally effective. The third need is therefore, to make employees effective in their performance through continuous training.

d. *Developing human skills:* Apart from emphasising on technical and conceptual skills, new training programmes also emphasise on developing human skills of employees. Such human skills are necessary for effective interpersonal relations and sustaining healthy work environment. This need for training, therefore, cannot be altogether ignored.

e. *Imparting trade specific skills:* In industrial employment, the convention is to recruit workers and employees through compulsory apprenticeship training. Such apprenticeship training enables an organisation to impart industry and trade specific skills to workers. This also, therefore, is an important need for manpower training.

f. *Stabilising work force:* Throughout the world importance of training is now increasingly felt for stabilising the work force to withstand the technological change and for making the organisation dynamic in this changed process. Management theorists now unanimously agree that it is the responsibility of the organisation to train and develop their manpower on a continuous basis.

5.1.3 Classification of Training Programmes

Depending on the functional level and occupational categories of employees, an organisation can classify training programmes as under:

Level	Types of Training	
1. Workers	(i)	Introduction
	(ii)	Job Training
	(iii)	Craft Training
	(iv)	Special Purpose Training
2. Supervisors	(i)	Induction
	(ii)	Foremanship / Shopfloor Supervision
	(iii)	Manpower Management
3. Staff Members	(i)	Induction
	(ii)	Professional
	(iii)	Technical
	(iv)	Human Relations
4. Managers and Executives	(i)	Induction
	(ii)	Executive Training
	(iii)	Training in Executive Development

Apart from the above routine training programmes for different levels, training on Total Quality Awareness and training encompassing all aspects of Total Quality Management has now become almost compulsory for all functional levels.

5.2 INDUCTION AND ORIENTATION

These terms are interchangeably used to give a friendly welcome to the new employees as members of the organisation as also to introduce the new employees with the available installations (plant and machineries, systems), work norms, organisational objectives and the job positions of the employees. Some organisations make available programmed instructions materials to new employees to help them to get acquainted with the departmental rules and regulations, their entitlement for leave, pay, overtime, retirement benefits and other miscellaneous privileges, which affect their whole service. Tata Iron and Steel Company circulate to all their employees, in addition, a brief booklet under the name and style of "Write your future in Steel" to illustrate their career prospects. However, such documented materials cannot be made available by all organisations. They try to supplement it through a brief induction programme.

5.2.1 Supervisory Training Programme

Supervisors monitor the work of the workers and are arms of management. They must have adequate skill, experience, ability and leadership. A supervisor is required to do job in five broad areas, i.e. knowledge of the work, awareness of responsibilities, capacity to instruct, skill in improving methods and ability to work with people.

The tentative contents of a supervisory training programme may be drawn after the charts of such contents prescribed by Earl Planty and William Mocorx as per chart given here in after.

5.2.2 Training for Top and Middle Management

Top and Middle Management personnel are trained mainly on following eight areas to expose them to the managerial practices:

1. *Planning:* This covers the policy, general programme and plans of the organisation and also methods for effective action.

2. *Control:* To check current performance against predetermined standards (as mentioned in the plans, to ensure progress and also to record experience from the working of plans to serve as guide to possible future operations.

3. *Coordination:* To balance the team efforts ensuring, proper allocation of activities among different members of the group.

4. *Motivation:* This covers employees' morale and given by proper leadership. The art of self-motivation has to be inculcated in the manager and executives.

5. *Inspiration.*

6. *Communication.*

7. *Decision.*

8. *Integration.*

Contents of Supervisory Training Programme

Administrative Training	Orientation Training	Human Relations Training	Technical Training	Teacher Training
Duties and responsibilities of a Supervisor. Basic principles of Industrial organisation. Discpline and control.	The company size, structure of organisation, history, market share, achievements, objective and mission. Product Training. Shop rules and regulations. Personnel Policies. Union Contract. Company Services. Service Departments.	Induction of new employees. Giving orders and directions. Communication. Developing Understanding. Correcting subordinates. Inculcating initiative and confidence. Placement and supervision. Job evaluation, Performance measurement and incentives. Reducing absenteeism and labour turnover. Self improvement Grievance handing. TQM, Small Group activities. Employee Empowerment.	Basic science, mathematics and statistics. Special Technical training. Trade training Training on Costing methods. Training on time study and other industrial engineering techniques. Production planning and control. Labour legislation. TQM and ISO: 9000	Instructor Training. Conference leadership.

5.2.3 Identification of Training Needs

Traditionally, training needs identification is left with HRD department. HRD department, to keep pace with organisational requirements used to identify series of training modules for different categories of employees and publish such training calendars to circulate among different departments to depute their employees for such training courses. Depending on the facilities available, some of these training courses are also offered utilising in-house training faculties, while for others (where expertise is not available) such training may either be offered by retaining professional trainers or by deputing employees to attend some outside training courses.

However, to ensure better utilisation of employees' acquired knowledge and skill, identification of training needs are now being left with the respective departmental heads, who because of their proximity with the employees concerned can better suggest the training and development needs. Hence, right at the beginning of the year, HRD department circulates the format for suggesting training requirements of different departments, which after necessary process, they develop as training calendars. Head of the department through performance appraisal, job evaluation and keeping in mind future requirement (due to change of technology, etc.), may identify such training requirements and also study the cost-benefit aspect closely monitoring employees' post-training performance.

Incidentally, it has now also become one important corporate practices in line with ISO Certification requirement.

5.2.4 Steps for Designing the Training Programme

The following steps are involved in designing the training programme:

1. *Selecting Strategies:* The first step is to choose a strategy or strategies for training methods. Strategies prioritise training objectives and also help in selecting training areas which may be skill formation, developing conceptual understanding, etc.

2. *Breaking Objectives:* The second step is to break the general training objectives into different parts like knowledge, understanding and skills. Each constituent part of the training objective is matched with appropriate training events.

3. *Choose Methods:* The next step is to use specifications for different training methods to decide over time and the facilities required for the programme as a whole.

4. *Deciding on Packages:* The fourth step is to decide different packages in which programmes could be offered. An organisation at this stage considers different training packages, keeping in view the time and cost aspects.

5. *Designing the Programme:* The final step is to design the training programme.

5.2.5 Sequence of a Training Programme

Any training programme should follow the order of sequence of actions as under to make it effective:

1. Designing the programme matching with the learning process.
2. Matching the programme to the organisational expectations.
3. Developing the training group.
4. Identifying the themes of training and development.
5. Achieving consistency in training.

5.2.6 Need for a Training Policy

To ensure consistency in Training and Development Function, the Personnel vis-a-vis each department of organisation develops a suitable training policy, defining the scope, objective, philosophy and techniques. Such a training policy, inter alia, serves the following purposes:

1. It defines what the organisation intends to accomplish through training.
2. It indicates the type of persons to be responsible for training functions.
3. It identifies the formal and informal nature of training.
4. It fixes training priorities and type of training needed.
5. It spells out the duration, time and place of training.
6. It indicates the need for engaging outside institutions for training.
7. It embraces and includes training in relation to labour policies of the organisation.

5.3 TRAINING METHODS

The following methods are mostly used for training of employees.

1. *On the Job training:* Under this technique an employee is put on the job and is trained to perform the said job thereby helping the employee to acquire the skills for performing the said job in future. Most of the organisations utilise the services of senior workers to impart such trainings. Apprenticeship, creation of assistant–to positions, job rotation and special assignments are different nature and forms of such training programmes.

2. *Job Instruction training:* This is a training through step by step learning. Usually steps necessary for a job are identified in order of sequence and an employee is exposed to the different steps of a job by an experienced trainer.

3. *Vestibule Training:* This method duplicates on the job situation away from actual worksite with machinery and equipment similar to those used in actual production or operation and is used to help employees to acquire new skills. Usually, training is given away from the production centre.

4. *Training Centre training:* Such site trainings are given in the form of lectures, conferences, case studies, role-playing and discussions.

5. *Simulation:* Simulation again duplicates the actual condition encountered on a job. The Vestibule training method or the Business game method are the examples of business simulation.

6. *Apprenticeship:* Such training is given for a longer duration to help the employees to acquire skills in specific trade(s). A major part of this training is given on the job.

5.3.1 Off-the-job Methods

These methods consist of the following:

    a. Lectures

    b. Conferences

    c. Group Discussions

    d. Case Studies

    e. Role Playing

    f. Programme Instruction

    g. T-Group Training

5.3.1A *Lectures*

Through lectures participants are motivated to learn. Lectures focus on understanding rather than enriching knowledge and skills through reading assignments and experience. However, empirical studies on the effectiveness of training through lecture methods indicate that this is not effective for obvious inability of participants to retain the information and failures of the trainers to make such sessions more interesting relating to on-the-job experience.

5.3.1B *The Conference method*

It is a participative group centred method through which participants develop knowledge and understanding by small group discussions and active participation.

5.3.1C *Group Discussions*

This is also a very useful method of training and is usually based on papers prepared by trainees on a given subject. The trainees read their papers which are usually followed by critical discussions. It may, however, be a follow-up discussion on some statement or on a paper presented by an expert.

5.3.1.D *Case Study:*

Case study method helps students to learn on their own by independent thinking. A set of data or some descriptive materials are given to the participants asking them to analyse, identify the problems and also to recommend solutions for the same.

5.3.1E *Role Playing*

This training method particularly helps in learning human relations skills through practice and imbibing an insight into one's own behaviour. Trainees of such programme are informed of a situation and asked to play their roles in such (imaginary) situation before the rest of the class. This, therefore, helps in the enriching of interactional skill of the employees.

5.3.1F *Programmed Instruction*

This method is pre-arranged desired course of proceeding to the learning or acquisition of specific skills or knowledge. Information in such programmes is conveniently broken into different units, to allow the trainees to learn at their convenient pace.

5.3.1G *T-Group Training*

T-group is sensitivity training that takes place under laboratory condition and is mostly instructional and informal kind of training. Trainer in such a training programme is a catalyst. He helps the individual participants to understand how others perceive his behaviour, how he acts to others behaviour and how and when a group acts either in a negative or in a positive way.

5.4 PERFORMANCE APPRAISAL

Performance means the degree or extent with which an employee applies his/her skill, knowledge and efforts to a job, assigned to him/her and the result of that application. Performance Appraisal means analysis, review or evaluation of performance or behaviour of an employee. It may be either formal or informal, oral or documented, open or confidential. However, in organisations we find formal appraisal system in documented form. It is, therefore, a formal process to evaluate the performance of the employees in terms of achieving organisational objectives.

Like any other personnel vis-a-vis HRD function, Performance Appraisal is also an important managerial activity.

5.4.1 Importance

For all important decisions concerning people, like transfer and promotion, remuneration, reward, training and development, so also for long-term manpower planning and organisation development, performance appraisal is necessary. A well documented performance appraisal system helps in understanding the attributes and behaviours of employees. It is also necessary for motivation, communication, strengthening superior- subordinate relationship, target fixing (key performance areas

/ key result areas), work planning and for improving the overall performance of the organisation.

5.4.2 Functions

The primary functions and objectives of performance appraisal are:

1. To identify and define the specific job criteria. Many organisations at the beginning of the year set Key Performance Areas (KPAs) or Key Result Areas (KRAs) for employees based on mutual discussions.

2. To measure and compare the performance in terms of the defined job criteria. KRAs and KPAs are also designed so as to help in measuring job performance in quantitative or qualitative terms.

3. To develop a justified reward system, relating rewards to the employees' performance.

4. To identify the strengths and weaknesses of employees and to decide on proper placement and promotion.

5. To develop suitable training and development programmes for enriching performance of the employees.

6. To plan for long term manpower requirements and to decide upon the organisational development programmes need, duly identifying the change areas (for over all improvement of the organisation).

7. To identify motivational reinforcers, to develop communication systems and also to strengthen superior-subordinate relationships.

5.4.3 Objectives

A Performance Appraisal system tries to serve various purposes and attain a number of objectives. The major objectives of Performance Appraisal system may be classified as remedial, developmental, innovative and motivational.

a. Remedial objectives aim at improving the performance of the individual employees which are not upto the required standard of the organisation.

b. Developmental objectives stimulate growth of the employees both in their present and future jobs. Thus, it identifies training and development needs, ensures placement and promotion, etc.

c. Innovative objectives are for discovering ways to deal with a new job and also to identify and develop better ways for existing jobs.

d. Motivational objectives are for rewards, motivations, effective communication and also for better interpersonal relations.

5.5 TYPES AND METHODS OF PERFORMANCE APPRAISAL

Different methods of performance appraisal are followed in different organisations to achieve the above objectives. Since some methods of performance appraisal are complicated and call for adequate knowledge in quantitative techniques, many organisations follow traditional methods of appraisal while other consider modern methods as the basics for evaluating job performance of their employees.

5.5.1 Traditional Methods

Traditional methods of performance appraisal may be categorised broadly under the following heads:

5.5.1A *Straight Ranking Method*

This is the oldest and simplest method of performance appraisal by which employees are tested in order of merit giving some numerical rank and placed in a simple grouping. Such grouping separates employees under each level of efficiency which may vary from most efficient to least efficient. Since it is a blunt quantification of performance, it does not account for behaviourial parameters and only considers an individual employee's level of efficiency in relation to others. For such obvious deficiency, this system does not provide scientific basis for performance appraisal of employees.

5.5.1B *Paired Comparison Techniques*

This is a somewhat better method of performance appraisal as each employee is compared with others in pairs at a time. For each performance trait, an individual employee's performance is tallied with others in pairs and then rank order is decided. This system is not suitable in those cases where number of employees are usually high. For better comprehension, a sample table of comparison on trait 'reliability' is presented below:

For Trait 'Reliability' Person Rated

As Compared to	A	B	C	D	E
A	X	~	~	~	~
B	X	+	~	+	~
C	+	~	X	+	~
D	+	~	+	X	~
E	+	+	~	+	X

5.5.1C *Man-to-Man Comparison*

Under this method certain factors are selected for analysis like leadership, initiative, inter-personal relationship, etc. and a scale is designed by a rater for each such factors. After rating such factors individually and accordingly, the aggregate performance of an individual employee having been decided, such aggregate performance is also given a scale. Likewise an individual employee is considered with others. This method is somewhat like factor comparison method widely used in job evaluation. Since developing uniform rating scale is a complicated task, this factor is not much in use in practice for performance appraisal of employees by organisations.

5.5.1D *Grading method*

Under this method certain features worth understanding the performance of an employee are identified. Such features may be leadership, communication power, analytic ability, job knowledge, etc. The raters mark/rate such features here also according to a scale and match an employee's performance compared to his own developed grade definitions. For example A, B, C, D, E – types of grade definitions for each feature may be developed by a rater to indicate, A = very significant, B = significant, C = moderate, D = average, E = poor. Such types of grading are of much use for selection of an employee or grading them in written examinations.

5.5.1E *Graphic or Linear Rating Scale*

Such rating scale is normally a continuous scale which enables a rater to mark somewhere along a continuum. Usually a printed form is given to a rater along with a factor to be rated, giving a continuous scale against each such factor. This method, therefore, enables quantification of performance scores and analysing its significance using statistical techniques. Since making a rating cluster is difficult for obvious difference in individual characteristics of each job the system may not always ensure objective appraisal.

5.5.1F *Forced Choice Description method*

It is a combination of objective and subjective judgement on an individual employee's performance against each rating element. Positive and negative phrases are given asking the rater to indicate applicability of such phrases as objectives in describing the employee whose performance is rated. For its obvious complexity this system is not much used.

5.5.1G *Forced Distribution method*

It is a method to evaluate employees' performance according to a pre-determined distribution scale. For example under such a method the rater is asked to distribute 5 per cent of the total employees on top of the scale, indicating their superior performance and promotability, 10 per cent may be put immediately under this level, indicating their good performance and future promotability. This system is easy to understand and can be applied to organisations without much hassles.

5.5.1H *Checklist method*

It is simply a process of reporting employees' performance compiling yes/no responses. Final rating is done by the Personnel vis-a-vis HRD department based on such reports. Since this is not an objective method of appraisal, it is not free from bias.

5.5.1I *Free Easy method*

It is an open ended qualitative appraisal of employees' performance, giving an opportunity to the rater to put down his impression in subjective form on important job factors. Since it is descriptive and essay type, it is likely to be biased and judgement errors may crop in.

5.5.1J *Critical Incident method*

This method measures employees' performance in terms of certain 'events' or 'critical incidents' instrumental for success or failure on the job. Such critical incidents are identified by the rater after indepth study of the employees' working. As negative incidents get more focused and recording for incidents demand for utmost care, it is not free from defects.

5.5.1K *Group Appraisal method*

It is an evaluation of an employee by multiple judges. The immediate supervisor of the employee and a few other discuss the performance standards and then evaluate the performance of the employee. The greatest advantage of this method is that it is relatively free from bias even though it is time consuming.

5.5.1L *Field Review method*

This type of review is conducted by the Personnel department by interviewing the supervisor of an employee to understand the subordinate employees performance. Normally, for such type of appraisal, the appraiser, i.e. the representative of the Personnel department gets equipped with certain questions and more in the form of informal interview, asks those questions about the employees, whose performances are to be reviewed to their respective supervisors. Since this process of appraisal is an indirect method it may not always reflect the true performance level of the subordinate employees since such an interview is always having a sensitising effect on the interviewee, whose responses may be some opinionated generalisations. Moreover, this method keeps the key managerial personnel always busy for appraisal. Despite such defects the process being simple and being possible to administer centralising the task of performance appraisal function, most of the organisations prefer to have this type of appraisal for lower level employees.

5.5.2 Modern Methods

The traditional methods of performance appraisal, discussed above, suffer from major limitation for their obvious emphasis on assessing individual performance or task considering it as an isolated factor. To eliminate such narrow and partial approach, the newer techniques of performance appraisal have been developed and are widely practiced by the organisations, particularly for managerial and supervisory employees. Some of the modern techniques are discussed below.

5.5.2A *Appraisal by Results or Management by Objectives*

Management by Objectives (MBO) is a comprehensive management approach which is adopted for performance appraisal and so also for organisational development. When MBO is used for performance appraisal only its primary focus is on developing objective criteria for evaluating the performance of the individuals. Identification of common goals is jointly done by the superior and subordinate managers of an organisation. After such identification each individual's major areas of responsibility are defined. Such defined responsibility later becomes the basis for evaluating the performance of the individual employee.

Most of the organisations emphasise on developing KRA's through MBO exercise, as this approach necessitates joint meeting of the supervisor and the employee to define, establish and set goals or objectives which the individual employees would achieve within a prescribed time limit (mostly it is in the form of yearly targets). Such an excercise also establish ways and methods to measure performance. Goals are mostly work related and career oriented and are integrated with over all organisational objectives. Periodic evaluation of employee's performance as done in terms of goals and if required goals may be revised. MBO also calls for superior-subordinate interaction and supportive role of the supervisor (which as well includes counselling /coaching)

However, MBO system lays more stress on tangible goals and hence intangible goals like morales, good inter-personal relations, committment to the job, etc. are often ignored. Moreover, MBO exercise is too much time and money consuming.

5.5.2B *Assessement Centre method*

This method is to test candidates in a social situation by a number of assesors, using a variety of criteria (which may be a paper-pencil test, interviews, in-basket exercise, business game, role playing incident or a leaderless discussion). The assessors or evaluators are drawn from experienced executives, working at different levels of management. Under this method performance of employees is evaluated both individually and collectively. This method is useful in measuring inter-personal skills, organising and planning ability, creativity, resistance to stress, work motivation, decision making power, etc.

5.5.2C *Human Asset Accounting method*

The method attaches money estimates in the value of manpower of an organisation. The process is somewhat like estimating the goodwill value and can be appraised by developing a procedure to undertake periodic measurement of certain variables. Such variables are either categorised as Key variables or Intervening variables. Key variables are policies and decisions of an organisation, its leadership strategies, skills and behaviour of an employee, etc. Intervening variables are loyalties, attitudes, motivations, interpersonal relations, communication and decision making. Measuring such variables over several years, quantification of human assets is difficult for the obvious problem in developing the accounting procedure. It is not a very popular method of performance appraisal. However, this system is more appropriately used for evaluating the collective performance of an organisation, rather than individual appraisal of an employee. The method is useful for organisational development as it helps in identifying the changed areas more scientifically than any other method.

5.5.2D *Behaviourally Anchored Rating Scales (BARS)*

This method helps in measuring and improving job performance more accurately. For each performance area some standard statements are provided. These are then put on the scales in BARS. While developing such BARS, group discussions are conducted to identify significant job dimensions that need to be evaluated. BARS may be of different types for different job dimensions. Normally BARS are presented vertically with scale points ranging from five to nine. Because of its behavioural orientation, it is condidered as the most useful technique of performance appraisal. Moreover, this system provides opportunity to both appraisee and appraiser to interact and participate in developing standards for each performance area. This system being time consuming and pain staking, despite its advantages, is avoided by organisations.

5.6 STEPS TO PERFORMANCE APPRAISAL

Irrespective of the methods applied for performance appraisal, its steps follow more or less a set pattern, which are listed as below:

   a. Establishment of performance standards. This is done mostly while developing job description.

   b. Communication of standards to the employees.

   c. Measurement of performance

   d. Comparison of performance with the job standards.

   e. Discussing the appraisal results with the employees.

   f. Initiating the corrective action, where necessary.

5.7 PERFORMANCE COUNSELLING

It is a process of advising an employee, listening to his problems and enabling him to find a satisfactory solution on his own. Performance counselling is a process to help subordinates to analyse their performance objectively. It helps in identifying training and development needs and also ensures improvement in future performance of an employee.

Primarily, performance counselling attempts to help an employee in the following ways:

   1. It helps an employee to understand his own strengths and weaknesses. More effective counselling sessions even enable employees to make their independent SWOT Analysis, i.e. opportunities and threats in achieving the performance can also be made clear to such employees for their independent analyses of performance.

   2. Since good performance counselling believes in giving feeback information about the employees' behaviour and performance, it helps in improving professional and inter-personal competence of employees.

   3. It helps in setting goals, formulating action plan for further improvement of employees.

   4. It helps the employees to identify different alternatives for dealing with problems.

   5. Good performance counselling session, being supportive and being empathetic, make employees feel encouraged to openly discuss their aspirations, conflicts and problems.

5.7.1 Conditions for effective Performance Counselling

Conditions for effective Performance Counselling may be listed as follows:

   1. A climate of mutual trust, confidence and openness need to be ensured at the outset.

   2. Climate should be such that it can ensure subordinates' free partcipation in the review process and also in their giving the correct feedback. This is important as counselling is not a one way process of communication, but a two-way traffic really.

3. The focus of performance counselling is on employee development. Employee development should not be considered isolated from other issues of performance appraisal, i.e. remuneration and rewards, promotion, motivation, etc.

5.7.2 Different phases of Performance Counselling

There are different phases of Performance Counselling Process. They are mentioned below:

1. *Rapport Building:* The first phase of performance counselling is Rapport building, i.e. establishing a climate of acceptance, support, openness, etc. Subordinates should be assured in this phase that their superiors are keenly interested in their development. A successful rapport building phase, therefore, generates confidence in the employees, which facilitates sharing openly their perceptions, problems, conscience, feelings, etc.

2. *Exploration :* In this phase, apart from visiting the employees and creating a climate of openness, the counsellors help the employees to understand their strengths, weaknesses, opportunities and threats. The success of this phase lies in making the employees discover all these on their own and at the same time initiate remedial measures independently.

3. *Action Planning :* Specific plans and actions for the development of employees are identified at this phase of performance counselling. The counsellor helps the employees to implement such action plans for effective results. For making such action plans acceptable, some counsellors prefer to develop the action plans exposing employees to a series of brainstorming sessions. This process enables the employees to develop the action plans independently.

5.7.3 Performance Counselling Process

The counsellor in performance counselling sessions should be an excellent listener. He should pay attention to the ideas, feelings and sentiments of the person being counselled. This enables the counsellor to understand and analyse the subordinate's concern. The effectiveness of performance counselling session, therefore, depends on efficiency in asking questions. The questions should be framed in such a way that they should try to seek constructive suggestions from the subordinate, should be open-ended and empathetic. The questions should not be critical or should not appear as if the intention of the counsellor is to test or evaluate the subordinate person.

Secondly, performance counselling process should ensure communication of feedback to the subordinates in such a manner so as to evoke constructive response from them. Since giving negative feedback is embarrassing, feedback should always be descriptive and non-evaluative. It should be focused on the behavioural attributes rather than on the subordinate himself. Feedback should be made more data based and suggestive. It should be continuous and verifiable.

5.7.4 Counselling Interview

Before beginning the counselling session, the counsellor needs to study subordinate's job responsibilities, his education, training and experience, job performance and his past jobs. He should make adequate planning of the discussion, the issues involved and determine the development need to be discussed with the employee.

The interview should be sincere, informal and friendly. The counsellor should explain the purpose of the discussion to the interviewee and also emphasise on the issue that the interview is essentially a two-way communication. The subordinates should be encouraged to discuss their own appraisals about themselves. The counsellor should focus on the strong points and encourage the subordinates to suggest their own developments. It is essential for the counsellor to reach agreement on development plans and also to summarise the points discussed in the session at the end of the interview. He should make record on plans mutually agreed to in the interview.

REVIEW QUESTIONS

1. Identify the need for manpower training in an organisation. What are the important purposes served by training?

2. List out training programmes for different levels of employees and elaborate at least two such types of training programmes for workers.

3. What are the steps involved in designing a training programme? What sequence of actions usually a training programme follows?

4. Do you think there is need for a training policy in an organisation? Briefly outline some of the areas which need to be focused in such a policy.

5. Develop at least three sample training modules for supervisors, duly pointing out their objectives, course of contents, eligibility of participants, duration, etc.

6. What are the different training methods available for an organisation? Which are the methods you recommend for white collared and blue collared, employees respectively?

7. Do you think recent economic liberalisation programme of the Government of India has made training function more important for an organisation? Elaborate your answer duly listing out important training areas in the context of changing environment.

8. Define Performance Appraisal. Briefly state its importance and objectives. What are the steps you would like to follow for appraising the performance of a managerial employee?

9. What are the different performance appraisal systems followed in an organisation? Select at least five methods and briefly discuss their strengths and weaknesses.

10. Traditional Performance Appraisal Systems emphasise on assessing the individual performance as an isolated factor. Briefly discuss the newer techniques of performance appraisal, critically reviewing the shortcomings of traditional system.

11. Discuss the effectiveness of MBO and BARS in performance appraisal. Develop KRAs for a Personnel Manager of an organisation and identify five important performance criteria for assessing the performance on a six point Behaviourally Anchored Rating Scales.

12. Critically review the performance appraisal system in India. Elaborate your answer visiting at least two organisations.

13. Develop a standard performance appraisal form for supervisors in an organisation, selecting at least ten factors for review. Recommend your proposed develment plans for such supervisors based on your review.

14. Briefly state the importance and objectives of performance counselling. What are the conditions for effectiveness of performance counselling?

15. Short Notes

    1. T-Group Training
    2. Role Playing
    3. Vestibule Training
    4. Simulation
    5. Orientation Programme
    6. Craft Training
    7. Human Skills
    8. Counselling Interview
    9. Assessment Centre Method
    10. Field Review
    11. Critical Incident Method
    12. Key Performance Areas

APPENDIX-I

MANAGERIAL APPRAISAL REVIEW FORM

APPRAISAL PERIOD : FROM   TO

I PERSONAL DATA :

Name	Designation	Grade
Personal No. Date of birth	Department	Division
Academic Qualifications	Years of Experience	
Professional Qualifications	In Present Organisation	
Professional Membership	Outside Present Organisation	
Date of Recruitment	Date of Last Promotion	

II APPRAISAL:

II A. Important Points

1. Assess the employee on his performance in his present position only.
2. Try not to allow personal prejudices to influence your appraisal. The rating should be as objective as possible.
3. Assess the ratee on his performance during the whole year. Do not allow isolated incidents or recent instances to bias your assessment.
4. Assess each factor independently, uninfluenced by the rating on the other factors.
5. Assess the ratee on all factors.
6. The rater and reviewer must initial in ink in the box against the most appropriate rating in each case.
7. All entries in this form should be handwritten in legible condition.

FACTORS	Rater	Reviewer		DEGREE
1. Knowledge of the Job All round knowledge of the job including concepts and techniques required and their application; know-how of the latest trends, developments and innovations in the field of work.			Excellent	Exceptional mastery of all phases of work. Has upto date knowledge of his field.
			Good	Thorough knowledge of job.
			Satis-factory	Adequate knowledge of job for the position he is occupying.
			Unsatis-factory	Poor knowledge of the job.

FACTORS	Rater	Reviewer		DEGREE
2. Planning of Work Scheduling of one's assignments in order to meet deadlines; setting of well defined targets; concentration of task priorities; ability to anticipate problems and take corrective action.			Excellent	Highly effective in setting of goals and their prioritisation. Anticipates problems and takes corrective action.
			Good	Effective in meeting tough deadlines most of the time.
			Satis-factory	Usually effective in meeting routine schedules.
			Unsatis-factory	Is indifferent to planning and cannot meet deadlines.
3. Ability to Achieve Results Utilisation and productivity of subordinates and resources; target achievement; follow-up system and co-ordination with departments : coping with sustained work pressures; quick response to special jobs without letting routine matters suffer; keeping superiors and subordinates informed about relevant jobs, problems and results			Excellent	Highly effective in organising resources and getting extraordinary results.
			Good	Achieves superior results and is able to withstand work pressures and crisis.
			Satis-factory	Achieves normal results expected of him through good organisation and follow-up.
			Unsatis-factory	Does not use available resources; does not achieve expected results.
4. Sense of Responsibility Ability to handle given assignments independently or with minimum supervision; degres of chasing or control required from superiors; setting of self targets and their completion; seeking information on problems; willingness to take a decision or do a job without passing the buck.			Excellent	Very high sense of responsibility; can handle assignments independently; displays rate initiative and drive.
			Good	Is willing to shoulder greater responsibility than the job demands; displays considerable initiative.
			Satis-factory	Takes on responsibilities of his job and copes with routine problems. Takes routine decisions.
			Unsatis-factory	Does assigned task reluctantly; requires constant direction and supervision.

FACTORS	Rater	Reviewer		DEGREE
5. Maintaining Discipline Sense of organisational discipline and ability to maintain it in the work force; punctuality; on the job presence; setting of personal example to subordinates; firmness and fairness in dealings with sub-ordinates, standards of cleanliness, safety and housekeeping in the work place; willingness to accept the consequence of unpleasant decisions made by superiors.			Excellent	Maintains high standards or organisational discipline and sets personal example to his men.
			Good	Achieves above average standards of discipline, safety and housekeeping is committed to decisions of superiors.
			Satisfactory	Meets and maintains expected standards of discipine and punctuality.
			Unsatisfactory	Is not punctual and is noted for unscheduled absence; talks loosely about superiors.
6. Getting along with People Clarity and effectiveness in communicating with superiors, peers and subordinates; handling of conflicts, level of maturity in dealing with bosses and peers, ability to take feedback and correct one self; skill in influencing others without arousing antagonism. Caring attitude towards colleagues and subordinates.			Excellent	Has a marked ability for fruitful interaction with people.
			Good	Is highly effective in understanding, relating and communicating with people.
			Satisfactory	Has the ability to communicate with people and influence them for good performance.
			Unsatisfactory	Finds it difficult to relate with bosses, peers or subordinates.
7. Teamwork and Cooperation Ability to work with colleagues, peers and other departments; kind of participation in meetings; degree of involvement in team projects; willingness to share one's resources with others in the department if needed; seeking and offering peer assistance; degree of sensitivity to group feelings and responses.			Excellent	Highly productive and successful in working with colleagues and peers.
			Good	Positive participation and integration with team.
			Satisfactory	Adequate commitment and contribution to team effort. Notable peer collaboration.
			Unsatisfactory	Does not function as a team member. Goes all out for himself. Tends to disrupt rather than contribute to team efforts.

FACTORS	Rater	Reviewer		DEGREE
8. Identification with the Company Sense of identification with the company's values and interests; concern for satisfaction of clients/customer needs; pursuit of excellence in performance; concern for cost reduction through optimum utilisation of men, materials of equipment; concern for preservation of company's property.			Excellent	Thoroughly identifies himself with company's values and interests and transmits them to peers and subordinates.
			Good	Is involved with and loyal to company's interests. Has a high sense of belongingness to the company.
			Satis-factory	Shows necessary concern for company's value and interests.
			Unsatis-factory	Low commitment to company's interests. Talks loosely about the company and has no belongingness to it.
9. Development of Subordinates Ability to guide subordinates in their work assignments; delegation of work; steps taken for training and development of subordinates; ability to get them to accept the challenge of higher responsibilities or targets.			Excellent	Gives very high priority to development of subordinates.
			Good	Takes positive steps for subordinate development like training and job enrichment/enlargement.
			Satis-factory	Shows concern for development of subordinates. Is able to motivate them.
			Unsatis-factory	Has no interest in the development of his subordinates.
10. Approach to Problem Solving Ability to seek alternative ways to solve a problem or meet a deadline within the rules of the company; flexible and practical approach; ability to cope with unusual problems and situations; generation of original ideas and enduring solutions to problems.			Excellent	Is extremely resourceful and has practical and original skill to solve problems.
			Good	Is flexible in approach and successful in finding solutions to many unusual problems.
			Satis-factory	Able to find solutions to routine problems; is receptive to new ideas.
			Unsatis-factory	Is upset when problems come. Fails to solve them.

III A. Training Plans

Please tick below selectively, the type of training courses which you think will help to improve the ratee's performance.

1.   Technical (please specify the area)

2.   Functional (Please specify the area)

3.   Computers

4.   Management Training

    a.   General Management Programmes

    b.   Total Quality Management

    c.   Problem Solving Skills

    d.   Communications Skills

    e.   Leadership Skills

    f.   Inter-personal/Behavioural Skills

    g.   Value Engineering

5.   Any other (please specify)

III B. Development Plans

What are your plans to develop the ratee? (e.g. special assignments, increased responsibility, etc.)

I have seen my performance appraisal for the year .... and it has been discussed with me with respect to my performance and development plans.

Date ....   Signature of the Ratee

IV. Checklist of Observable Behaviour

Please go through each of the items listed below. Whenever the item description distinctly tallies with the observable behaviour in the ratee, tick in the column marked YES. If it is not so, please tick in the column marked NO. This checklist is not an assessment of performance. It is to be used for developmental purposes.

Sl. No.	Description	YES	NO
1.	Pays attention to documentation. Is systematic in record keeping for future references.		
2.	Is clear and concise in written communication.		
3.	Has the capacity for self-analysis and correction of his weaknesses. Is open to negative feedback.		
4.	Has the aptitude for systematic and methodical work. Is patient with minute details.		
5.	Makes positive attempts to update himself in his professional field and learn new things.		
6.	Does not accept sub-standard work.		

7.	Does not lose heart inspite of failures or setbacks.		
8.	Has a sense of humour.		
9.	Promotes healthy industrial relations in his department or work place.		
10.	Is skilled in organising complex activities.		
11.	Is trustworthy. Does not let down colleagues for personal gain.		
12.	Has the courage of his convictions. Express dissent where he is of a different approach to the task or problems.		
13.	Respectful of elders and superiors. Polite. Does not hurt colleagues or subordinates.		
14.	Finds it very easy to get to know people and get along with them.		
15.	Clear in his verbal communication. Is seldom misunderstood. Can convery his thoughts precisely and clearly.		

V. Confidential Rating of Overall Performance

Please initial in any one of the following	
The individual has achieved an exceptionally high standard of performance. In significant areas of responsibillity, he has exceeded expected standards. Performance is consistently excellent.	Outstanding
The standard of performance has been consistently above aggregate in several areas, responsibilities were discharged so as to merit favourable comment rather than mere statisfaction.	Superior
The individual has performed well by and large and to the satisfaction of his superior.	Satisfactory
Not upto the minimum requirements of the position.	Unsatisfactory

This employee has worked under my supervision

from _____   to _____

Signature of Rater   Date _____
Designation
Department

Signature of the Reviewing Authority   Date_____
Designation
Department

Strengths and Weaknesses of Different Performance Appraisal Methods

Methods	Strengths	Weaknesses
1. Appraisal by objectives (MBO etc.)	1. It provides a quantitative measurement of performance which is verifiable. Quantification of performance being objective, subjectivity in analyses can be avoided. 2. Weak performance area can be quickly identified, thus it provides a meaningful basis for improving the performance.	1. Appraisal being result oriented, it is not suitable for determining the potential. 2. Individual performance areas being different, it does not facilitate peer comparison.
2. Graphic Rating	1. It is a simple and popular method. 2. It facilitates peer comparison, therefore it provides an objective basis for decision on remuneration, rewards and promotion. 3. Certain common criteria may be provided for improving the quality of comparison.	1. Highly subjective and unreliable. 2. Being subjective, weighting of factors may be necessary for improving the quality of analysis. 3. It does not provide facility for feedback and employee development.
3. Essay Type	1. Its proper use can provide quality information which can help in taking meaningful decisions for placement, promotion and development.	1. It requires good writing ability 2. Appraisers should have the power to take mature judgement. 3. Being subjective, inter-employee comparison is difficult.
4. Critical incidents method	1. Being highly objective, it provides factual data on employee's performance and behaviour. 2. Usually helps in improving the commu-nication and development of employees. 3. It is useful as a supportive evaluation.	1. Since performance is analysed on incidents, it tends to be fragmentary. 2. It can't be an indepdent method of evaluation. 3. It does not provide any basis for comparison.

5. Forced Distribution	1. It is free from any bias and is uniform in standards.	1. It can't also be an independent method of appraisal. It is better used as a control instrument. 2. Not suitable for communication and employee development
6. Straight Ranking Method	1. It is simple and helps in taking decisions on salary progression and promotion.	1. It does not provide feedback and also it cannot be used for large groups and inter-departmental comparision.

APPENDIX-3

BEHAVIOURALLY ANCHORED RATING SCALE
GUIDE TO PERFORMANCE APPRAISAL

ASSESSMENT CRITERIA	A	B	C	D	E
1. QUALITY	Leaps tall buildings single bound	Must take running start to leap over tall building	Can only leap over a building with no spires	Needs some improvements	Can not recognise buildings at all. Much less jump
2. TIMELINESS	Is faster than a speeding bullet	Is as fast as a speeding bullet	Not as fast as speeding bullet	Would you believe a slow bullet?	Wounds self with bullet
3. INITIATIVE	Is stronger than a loco-motive	Is stronger than a bull elephant	Is stronger than a bull	Shoots the bull	Smells like a bull
4. ADAPTABILITY	Walks on water consistently	Walks on water in emergencies	Washes with water	Drinks water	Passes water in emergencies
5. COMMUNI-CATION	Talks with God	Talks with the Angel	Talks with himself	Argues with himself	Loses the arguments

6 MANAGEMENT SUCCESSION AND DEVELOPMENT

LEARNING OBJECTIVES

This chapter will help in developing:

☐ the concept of Succession Planning

☐ characteristics of Management Development

☐ objectives, purpose and steps in Management Development Programmes (MDP)

☐ a review of audit of MDP

☐ a focus on MDP in India

☐ characteristics and goals of Organisational Development (OD)

CONTENT OUTLINE

6.1 INTRODUCTION

Growth and survival of the organisation are the responsibilities of the top management. To fulfil such responsibilities each organisation needs to plan management succession. Succession planning is done in different time frames to ensure the availability of right managerial personnel at the right time in right positions for continuing organisation vitality and strength. Most of the organisations plan for immediate requirements matching with their budgets and business plans. This short sightedness leads them to an alarming situation, when they find shortage of managerial manpower to man different positions in the organisation, resulting in organisational collapse. To avoid this, good organisations try to make succession planning in three different time frames, i.e. Immediate (within 1 year), Intermediate (1 to 5 years) and Long-range (beyond 5 years). Prevailing managerial attitude, i.e. a potential threat from successor, which may not sustain the desire of the managers to cling to their chairs, also stands against the success of the succession planning.

6.2 STEPS IN SUCCESSION PLANNING

The first step is to prepare and develop a management staffing plan for all anticipated needs in different time frames. For important positions at the top managerial level, such planning should be done even for shorter duration, keeping in view the potential threat from eventual natural wastages (death, disability, premature retirement, etc.) and so also from job switch and change (which has now increased many times for obviously enhanced scope of job mobility). Other effects of external factors like economic factors, overall manpower factors should also be considered while making such plan. Each organisation has to review their business plans. Effect of such plans on managerial needs also need to be studied.

The second step is staffing and development . Staffing is concerned with recruitment, selection and placement. Selection and placement may be either done from outside or from within the organisation through promotion and transfer. Development of managerial personnel is done through training, job rotation, creating 'Assistant-to' positions, projects and board assignments, performance appraisal, counselling and guidance. In many organisations management adopts what they call grooming process for filling up important managerial positions. A manager is 'groomed by' giving temporary assignment, attaching him/her with the higher officer or sometimes designating the potential promotee as 'officer-on-special duty'.

The third step is to ensure congenial organisational environment to retain the desired managerial personnel. Unless this is done, the whole exercise of developing a successor may have to be repeated.

The fourth step is to develop a good performance appraisal system to get feedback on managerial performance and to review their progress and shortfalls.

Preparation of Management Resource Inventory is the final step in the succession planning. Such inventory contains details of personal data, performance records, skills, potential, career goals and career paths of managerial personnel.

Following the above steps, therefore, we can identify right managerial personnel for staffing present and future managerial vacancies.

6.3 MANAGEMENT DEVELOPMENT

It is a scientific training process for managers and executives to enrich their knowledge and skills, so as to make them competent to manage their organisations effectively. Unlike general purpose training, Management Development Programmes aim at developing conceptual and human skills of managers and executives through organised and systematic procedure. In India, many professional institutes, like Administrative Staff College of India, Management Development Institute, Indian Institute of Training in Industrial Engineering, etc. conduct different management development programmes to sensitise managers and executives to different emerging problems of corporate world. Most of the programmes being on general purpose issues, some corporate houses have also designed their own Management Development Programmes for their managers and executives.

In private sector Tata Management Development Centre (TMDC) at Jamshedpur conducts such programmes for Tata executives. In public sector, the Steel Authority of India Limited (SAIL) has its fullfledged management development centre at Ranchi, Kirloskar Group, Reliance Group and Lakshmi Group (Madras) are now developing their own management development centres to train their executives on general and organisation specific issues. In addition, in-house training divisions of business houses are also growing with requisite infrastructure to train their executives, in an attempt to reduce their dependence on outside agencies.

6.3.1 Characteristics of Management Development

To understand the concept of Management Development better, it is important to list out its characteristics:

a. *A continuous process:* Management Development is a continuous process. It should encompass the entire professional career of managers and executives. So long in India, management development used to be considered as a sporadic activity, resulting in its failure to meet the organisational requirements. In Japan, Zen Philosophic base facilitates to consider management development and the training function as a systematic and continuous activity of any organisation.

b. *Acknowledge updating activity:* The imperative need for management development should be appreciated as there always exists a gap between actual performance and potential performance. This, therefore, provides scope for continuous improvement in all functional areas. Management Development Programmes always attempt to bridge this gap enriching the functional capacity of executives and managers, continuously updating their knowledge and skill. The gap between potential capacity and actual capacity is always high for managers and executives across the world as knowledge and skill can never get plateaued.

c. *A vehicle for attitudinal change:* Human behaviour is dynamic. Its complexity can be appreciated once management development programmes are attempted to understand the behavioural and attitudinal aspects through stimulating sessions. Better interpersonal skill is an important pre-requisite for managerial success, which can be ensured through properly designed management development programmes.

d. *A stimulant to higher competence:* Unless managers and executives are stimulated to the intricacies of managerial stress/strain through different management development programmes, their full potentiality cannot be exerted for the benefit of the organisation. Management development programmes can be designed considering such issues like employees' motivation, habits, age-mix, pattern of conflict and chaos and this can enable elevation of managers 'functional competence' in an organisation.

e. *A feedback mechanism:* Management development programmes are designed after clear cut objectives and goals which enable the organisation to measure its effectiveness through a feedback mechanism, monitoring the functions of the executives during post-training phase.

f. *A deficiency improver:* Management development programmes are catered to the individual requirements to improve the functional deficiencies of the individual managers, thus, enabling the organisation to derive immediate benefits from such programmes.

g. *A self-development process:* Management development facilitates self development of managers as they learn many things through action learning methods, sharing the experience of each other in a stimulated class-room atmosphere.

6.4 COMPONENTS OF MANAGEMENT DEVELOPMENT PROGRAMMES (MDP)

Analysing the characteristics, we can identify three important components of MDP, i.e. selection, intellectual conditioning and supervised training.

Selection process enables us to understand the innate potentiality of the executives and the degree and extent of their managerial abilities.

Intellectual conditioning is the process of educating managers and executives on different managerial tools and techniques.

Supervised training, on the other hand, is the process of guiding managers and executives while they apply and use their knowledge in day to day work.

6.4.1 Steps of Management Development Programmes (MDP)

Steps of a good MDP may be listed as follows:

1. To look at the organisation's objectives,
2. To ascertain the development needs,
3. To appraise the present performance,
4. To prepare manpower inventory,
5. To plan for individual development programmes,
6. To establish training and development programmes,
7. To evaluate different programmes as above.

6.4.2 Objectives and Purpose of Management Development Programmes

Objectives and purposes of management development programme can be better understood in the context of changing requirements of the environment which constantly interacts with the business. Many Indian organisations have now been exposed to the problem of a major restructuring to respond to the economic liberalisation programmes of the government. Such programmes of the government are now compelling the Indian managers to face the challenge of competition, survive under economic uncertainty, take decisions, move quickly, shoulder the risk, improve the quality of work life, making organisations more socially responsive and transparent, etc. Market globalisation is also compelling Indian organisations to update their technology. Management philosophies are also constantly changing, particularly in the context of development of the concept of Total Quality Management (TQM), which inter alia calls for employee empowerment, total participation, small group activities like quality circles, attitudinal change of the managers cutting across structural barriers, etc. Change in public policies, increased consumer awareness, increased social and institutional requirements (pollution control, etc.), labour relations, etc. are also compelling the organisations to introduce Management Development Programmes for their managers and executives for renewing their knowledge and skills. The primary objective of Management Development Programme, therefore, is to make the executives and managers vis-a-vis the organisations socially responsive and managerially competent to survive in an atmosphere of uncertainty.

In addition, management development programmes also aim at achieving the following objectives:

a. To make available managers and executives with requisite knowledge and skill to meet the present and anticipated future needs of the organisations.

b. To encourage managers to develop their full potentiality for handling greater responsibility.

c. To improve the functional competence of the managers, making them more transparent and responsive to the changing needs of the organisation.

d. To sustain good performance of the managers throughout their careers, not to allow them to develop managerial obsolescence.

e. To develop managers for higher assignment, duly replacing the elderly executives.

However, such objectives of MDP vary for various levels of management. Their commonality for all levels is to infuse:

1. Attitudinal Change.
2. Behavioural Change
3. Change in knowledge and skills
4. Change in performance
5. Change in desired operational results.

Personal characteristics, level of intelligence and learning efforts of people at different managerial levels being different for each level, their exist different sets of objectives, which an organisation should strive to achieve.

6.4.3 MDP Objectives for Top Management

For top management , such objectives are mostly general, primarily intended to develop their understanding and decision making power. Such objectives can be listed as below:

1. To improve the thought process and analytical ability so as to enable the top level managers to understand the problems and take managerial decisions for the best interest of the organisations in particular and the country in general.

2. To broaden the outlook in regard to their role, position and responsibilities in the organisation and outside.

3. To think through the problems that control an organisation at present or might arise in the future.

4. To understand economic, technical and institutional forces to solve business problems and

5. To acquire knowledge about the problems of human relations.

6.4.4 MDP for Middle-level Management

For middle level management, MDPs are intended to develop their intellectual faculty and at the same time to improve their decision making power with some knowledge of specialised fields. However, such objectives can be listed as follows:

1. To establish a clear picture of executive functions and responsibilities.

2. To bring an awareness of the broad aspects of management problems and an acquaintance with and appreciation of interdepartmental relations.

3. To develop the ability to analyse problems and to take appropriate action.

4. To develop familiarity with the managerial uses of financial accounting, psychology, business law and business statistics.

5. To inculcate knowledge of human motivation and human relationships.

6. To develop responsible leadership.

6.4.5 For Functional Executives and Specialists

1. To increase functional knowledge in specific fields in which the executive works like marketing, production, finance, personnel, etc.

2. To increase proficiency in different management techniques like work study, inventory control, operations research, quality control, etc.

3. To understand different functions in a company.

4. To understand human relations problems and

5. To develop the ability to analyse problems in one's area of function.

However, without favourable climate in the organisation, MDP cannot attain the desired objectives. Every organisation should have well defined policy for the development of managers.

6.4.6 Techniques of Management Development

Planning MDP deserves utmost attention and importance. The objectives of the programmes need to be defined at the outset. Objectives may either be to impart knowledge and skills for more effective functioning of the managers in their present positions or to equip them for holding higher positions in future. Most of the organisations through adequate career planning work out promotion paths for maragers. Unlike career planning programme for non-managerial employees, which show such career progress path in similar or allied job families, MDP may even chalk out career planning for managers and executives in different functional areas cutting across departmental barriers. Good MDPs are carefully planned so as to give responsibilities to each executive to prepare for replacement in successive grades.

6.4.7 Job Rotation

Another technique of MDP is to plan a systematic and deliberate assignment of managerial personnel, carefully selected by a top management committee into a series of positions. This device makes it possible to diversify the experience of the executives in a variety of activities. This method attempts directly to broaden the vision of administrators, developing the perspective on the total organisation. The period of their movement from job to job depends on their individual need and future prospects. They learn mostly by observation and practice which comes through substituting for vacationing managers.

There are different types of job rotation which may be for specified observation, assignment, managerial training positions or for unspecified managerial positions.

The system is criticised mainly for its high cost and 'jack-of-all-trade' type development. It defers specialisation and also lowers job efficiency at new post.

6.4.8 'Assistants-to' Position

'Assistant-to' positions at executive level is a variation of job rotation system. This helps to broaden experience of executives exposing them to many areas of managerial practice. The success of such arrangements, however, depends upon the ability and willingness of the superiors to pass on the qualities to the successors, its adequacy, superiors' extent of up-to-date knowledge and talents and finally on the efforts of the subordinate officers to learn with utmost sincerity.

6.4.9 Projects and Boards

Another practical method of Management Development is to put management personnel on special projects or committees to provide them opportunities to analyse and solve actual problems facing top management. Since the executives encounter different sets of problems in dealing with such projects and boards, it broadens their perspective and inculcate confidence and a sense of responsibility in them. However, unless the executives are allowed to take time necessary to become experts, its purpose may get defeated.

Other techniques of MDP have been discussed earlier.

6.5 AUDITING THE MDP

John M. Elliott, Vice President of Dale, Elliott and Company, Inc., New York identified 15 aspects, more in the form of questions, to determine the functioning and effectiveness of MDP. These are as follows:

1. Identification of organisation's different job levels for establishing promotional channels for managers and at the same time determining the likely job vacancies at each level.

2. Determining whether enough promotable manpower are available at each level to fill all managerial openings, the possibility of filling such vacancies through organisation's own (internal) manpower, the extent of hiring from outside or to determine the queuing problem for promotable executives.

3. Whether career planning at all levels adequately meets financial and other long range growth plans.

4. Whether organisation is able to get flow of management trainees through annual campus interview.

5. Whether proper utilisation of employee's knowledge and skills is ensured.

6. Identification of specific job assignments, which will contribute most to prepare outstanding men for key jobs in the company.

7. Whether organisation can afford to retain potential executives on a particular job assignment for a long time to allow him to prove his ability to handle it competently.

8. Whether scheduling of the job assignment have been designed to round up experiences and training to enable the executives to mature ultimately to head a division or a department.

9. Whether a sufficient number of intermediate level jobs have been reserved as training spots for effecting job rotation or committee/board assignment.

10. Whether adequate recruitment facility exists to ensure that best talents are available for managerial vacancies including the positions of management trainees.

11. Whether best available tools and procedures including psychological test and interview guides have been developed to identify the potentiality of the executives.

12. Whether the organisation is taking full advantage of outside training facilities such as seminars and courses available through universities and professional bodies, so also whether in-house training facilities have been well equipped to train the executives to enable them to develop their potential knowledge and skills.

13. Whether every potential managerial personnel is working under a superior, who is able to give guidance, counsel and also able to instill confidence and sense of responsibility.

14. Whether adequate feedback system exists to review and update MDP time to time depending on changing requirements.

15. Whether a comprehensive guide book has been developed for use of all senior managers for the success of MDP. Such a guide book comprises of the following sections.

    a. The objectives of the programme

    b. Characteristics needed in a managerial trainee

c. Job scheduling procedure

d. Training, Consulting, etc.

Answers to the above check-list of MDP enables us to understand the effectiveness or otherwise of MDP.

6.5.1 Why does MDP fail in most of the organisations

Most of the business organisations fail to provide an environment which can encourage, nurture and promote the growth of management development, i.e. a climate which can support it rather than to oppose it. The following reasons may be listed for failure of management development programmes.

a. Purpose of the management development efforts in most of the organisations are often characterised by insincerity. They conduct it as a matter of ritual rather than a systematic one. Some organisations also arrange MDP for their executives only to enable them to enjoy a paid vacation.

b. Some organisations are too much concerned to get the immediate benefits of MDPs. They always concern themselves with the immediate pay-out and select MDPs which are designed only to impart business like knowledge rather than giving philosophic ideas or conceptual insights.

c. Organisations retain the services of consultants and professional trainers to conduct MDPs for their executives. Such an arrangement often suffers from practical happenings in the organisations, as such professional trainers and the consultants do not get adequate information about the functioning of the organisation for whom the programmes are designed for absence of interaction with such outside agencies. MDPs suffer from major limitations like impracticability in introduction, irrelevance, etc.

d. In some cases, lessons imparted in MDPs go in direct conflict with the philosophy of the organisation. Such incongruence, therefore, becomes a source of immediate frustration for the executives as they confront different situations in the respective organisations.

e. There is no system to evaluate the effectiveness of the MDPs by such outside agencies. Post-training evaluation system, in the form of scientific feedback mechanism, therefore, is considered essential for success of such programmes.

6.6 MANAGEMENT DEVELOPMENT PROGRAMMES IN INDIA

Some emerging issues

"Take away my factory, machinery, money and all that I have, but leave my MEN and I will re-build my industrial empire stronger and better."

–Henry Ford

The above statement amply emphasises the need for developing human resources of an organisation as a part of organisational strategy.

The Government of India has now gone in for major economic restructuring with a view to consolidating its position in the world market and achieving internal economic balance and growth. Liberalisation in terms of major changes in the industrial policy, as a part of the economic restructuring programmes, had brought in a lot of competition for the over-protected Indian industrial organisations in general. Allowing free flow of foreign capital and direct participation of multinational organisations in the corporate sector have made the Indian industrial organistions exposed to intense competition.

Effect of such liberalisation on the domestic front of the Indian industrial organisations have again been multiplied by certain developments at the international plane which are more in the form of global trade restrictions. Certification as per the quality-system standards (developed by the International Organisation for Standardisation) of the products of the Indian industrial organisations is now almost essential for going global. Total Quality Management (TQM) is now a widely discussed issue in the corporate world.

Major economic restructuring at the macro level and the global changes taken together have prompted the Government of India to start with a National Renewal Fund (NRF) in order to give effect to the Exit Policy on one hand and to upgrade the skills of the employees retained through intensive training on the other. Organisations, in order to trim their employees, will hence forth have to implement Voluntary Retirement Schemes (VRS) by making extra payments by way of compensation (Exit Incentive) in addition to the normal statutory payments. The remaining employees (who do not opt for VRS) will now have to be trained vigorously in order to adapt them to the changed job requirements, vis-a-vis upgradation of technology, modernisation and restructuring of jobs.

In the above backdrop, training as a managerial function, in the corporate sector in India, has become very important. The training departments (where they exist) are now busy in designing and developing training programmes even for the employees at the lowest level with a view to equipping them for getting suitably redeployed vis-a-vis restructuring of jobs.

Training the employees on TQM strategy at a time when the Indian economy has gone in for major restructuring has assumed much importance primarily because today a corporate organisation in India cannot expect to survive merely by developing a strategic plan based only on extrapolation of production and profit figures. It has to survive in highly competitive environment both at the domestic and the global fronts. Thus restructuring of the production process, based on technological dynamism, in an organisation has become imperative. Economic restructuring at the macro-level has an inevitable impact on the production process in an organisation at the micro-level. Restructuring of a production process, as a natural consequence of economic restructuring, necessitates restructuring of manpower in an organisation. Since trimming of surplus employees in an organisation by offering them 'golden handshake' under the VRS is restricted only to those who opt for that, the only other effective way open is to redeploy the surplus employees after intensive need based training.

Keeping in mind the important performance areas in TQM Startegy in the corporate sector, training programmes are arranged for all categories of employees. Such training programmes are usually on:

1. Total Quality Awareness
2. Product Familiarisation

3. Process Familiarisation

4. Multiple-skill Development

5. Simple Problem Solving Techniques

6. Statistical Process Control

7. Quality Circle Concepts and

8. Total Productive Maintenance

The duration of each training programme varies from one week to two weeks depending on the participant's level and power of understanding.

For managers and executives, TQM techniques inter alia call for appreciating these issues:

a. Formal education and age are not really the factors, that determine the effectiveness or otherwise of learning of TQM techniques. TQM techniques essentially have their roots in basic humanism. The conceptual and technical aspects of TQM can only be appreciated at a deeper level if training programmes on TQM genuinely have the humanistic tone.

b. Attitudinal changes at the top are important to operationalise TQM in an organisation. Unless the top level personnel change their attitudes, e.g. accepting a flatter organisation structure, following an egalitarian approach, becoming receptive to change on a continuous basis, encouraging participative management and supporting group performance, it is not really possible to inculcate TQM culture in an organisation.

The emerging issues for designing MDPs in India, therefore, can be listed as follows:

1. Developing culture-specific management programmes, to appreciate humanistic tone of TQM techniques. This dimension of TQM techniques were incorporated with rare precision and clarity in a number of ancient Indian texts, which are grossly misunderstood as ethico-religious.

Teachings of the *Ramayana* have, inter alia, underscored the role of enthusiasm as driving force in all human endeavours. Similarly, the *Srimad Bhagawat Gita* has emphasised the significance of mutuality and cooperation in all spheres of human life. One of the important messages of the *Srimad Bhagawat Gita* is that the imminent role of man in the work environment can be effective, provided it continues to be guided in the light of a transcendent perspective about work. Importance of group performance and participative management have also been focused in the *Ramayana* and *Mahabharata*. Indian psycho-philosophy recognises that each human being is spontaneously bestowed with perfection within.

2. Appreciating corporate practices and social systems in India while designing MDPs. Jobs in Indian industrial organisations are not specialised and fractionised to replace intuition and ingenuity of the employees in general. Employees, in their limited spheres, always make use of their craftsmanship with a view to resolving technical problems in different activity areas. Tracing back history, we find that the Indian social system had definite orientation towards developing and maintaining different social groups in terms of certain crafts. The quality elements in a particular craft and the skills necessary were deciding

factors for the purpose of ranking the craft along with others in order of importance. There was a time when goldsmiths, carpenters and weavers were the craftsman-groups in India who enjoyed the highest status. In the later years, however, human aspects of social functioning in India gradually lost importance.

The future management development programmes in India, therefore, cannot merely sustain on traditional skill upgradation, conceptual or technical issues but most of other general culture specific and human issues to develop human resources will be required to translate the challenges of change into reality. This is the only reason why many management development programmes now emphasise on human dimensions.

6.7 ORGANISATIONAL DEVELOPMENT

Significance of organisational development (OD) has also been discussed in brief in Chapter 1. But as an important sub-system of HRD, here again we are discussing this in detail.

Organisation Development is a strategy or an effort, which is planned and managed from the top, to bring about planned organisational changes for increasing organisational effectiveness through planned interventions based on social philosophy.

The following statement amply clarifies the need for OD in an organisation:

> *"Circumstances of an ever-changing market and an ever-changing product are capable of breaking any business organisation if that organisation is unprepared for change-indeed, in my opinion, if it has not provided procedures for anticipating change".*

> **–Alfred P. Solan**

6.7.1 Characteristics of OD

a. *Planned Organisation Change:* It involves identification of the problem, diagnoses the organisation, develops strategies for improvement. The variables considered by organisation development programmes are – values. attitudes, organisation culture and team development.

b. *Planned Intervention:* It is a planned intervention in the existing organisation that helps it to become more viable. It, therefore, examines present working norms, values and possible areas of conflict of the organisation and develops alternatives for its better health. The interventionist needs to diagnose different sub-systems of the organisation and develops alternatives for its better health. The important areas of intervention are planning and decision making processes, goal setting, team development, organisation structure, values and cultural norms, organisation culture and upgrading employees' skills and abilities.

c. *Top Management Commitment to OD:* Top management should feel interested in the programme and its outcome and effectively support efforts in this direction. Unless mutual trust and collaborative relationships are developed between the change agents (which in most of the cases are consultants or professionals) and the management of the enterprise, organisation development efforts may not succeed.

d. *Social Philosophy as a Norm of Change:* Bureaucratic model of organisation ignores the basic human factors and thereby reduces organisational effectiveness. The interventionist, therefore, requires to use the behavioural science knowledge and develop a system which is more human and democratic.

6.7.2 Organisation Development and Management Development

Organisation Development, however , should not be confused with Management Development. Management development is virtually development of managers. Management development, therefore, is concerned with upgrading of managers' skills and abilities whereas organisation development, though includes management development , is primarily concerned with improving the total system constituting the organisation.

6.7.3 Goals of Organisation Development

The important goals of OD are as follows:

1. To emphasise the need for changing from the close system to open system by inculcating various changes in the organisation. Such changes inter alia, also include introduction of concepts of social philosophy in the organisation which makes the organisation socially more responsible and transparent.

2. To supplement authority and hierarchical role with knowledge and skill, replacing traditional authority assigned role, which creates a more congenial work environment.

3. To build mutual trust and confidence in the organisation for man managing and reducing conflict.

4. To change structure and roles inconsistent with accomplishment of goals.

5. To encourage sense of ownership and pride in the organisation.

6. To decentralise decision making close to the source of activity.

7. To emphasise on feedback, self-control and self-direction.

8. To develop the spirit of cooperation, mutual trust and confidence.

9. To develop reward system based on achievement of goals and development of people.

It is apparent from the above discussion that the goal of OD is basically to change the attitudes of people in the organisation so as to enable them to identify the change areas and implement the desired organisation changes on their own.

6.7.4 Steps in Organisation Development

Robert Black and Jane S. Mouton (1963) suggested six phase approach to Organisational Development as under.

1. Investigating by each member of the organisation of his own managerial styles,

2. Examination of boss-subordinate relationship,

3. Analysis of work team action,

4. Exploration of coordination issues of inter related terms,

5. Identifying and defining major organisational problem areas and

6. Planning for executing agreed upon solutions that result changes in the organisation.

However, OD effort progresses through a series of well defined stages, which can be enumerated as follows:

a. ***Identification and diagnosis of the problem:*** Required changes in relation to various units in the organisation should be identified and diagnosed duly examining the feedback from employees. Effective identification and diagnosis of the problem should be preceded by an employee survey.

b. ***Developing of strategy:*** While developing appropriate strategy, it is necessary to study people, sub-system and organisation as a total system. Strategy is the direction and scope of an organisation in the long run matching resources and changing environment.

c. ***Implementing the programme:*** OD programme should be implemented in a phased manner, i.e. it should be tried at the outset only in small part of the organisation and on getting positive results only it should gradually be implemented in the total organisation. Since total organisational change precede attitudinal change, change in values and beliefs of the people , the initial thrust should be given to training of employees, improvement of their skill developing self-awareness, improving inter-personal relationships, reducing conflict, etc.

d. ***Reviewing the progress of the programme:*** Review of OD programme should be preferably done by a qualified person who was not involved in designing and developing the OD programme for getting unbiased opinion.

REVIEW QUESTIONS

1. Define Succession Planning. Enumerate the steps involved in Succession Planning.

2. What is Management Development? Outline the characteristics of Management Development.

3. What are the objectives and purposes of Management Development Programme? Do you think such objectives are different for different level of employees?

4. What important steps you consider necessary for designing a Management Development Programme? What are the techniques you recommend for Management Development?

5. What are the important aspects to be considered while auditing the Management Development Programme?

6. What are the reasons for failure of Management Development Programmes in India? What are your suggestions for making Management Development Programmes effective?

7. What is Organisation Development? What are its important characteristics? How does it differ from Management Development?

8. Write a short note on culture-specific management.

7 TRANSFER, PROMOTION AND JOB ROTATION

LEARNING OBJECTIVES

This chapter explains:

☐   the concept of transfer, promotion and job rotation

☐   different forms of transfers and promotions

☐   limitations of transfer

☐   purposes and basis of promotion

☐   the concept of job mobility, job enrichment, job enlargement and lateral and horizontal transfer

CONTENT OUTLINE

7.1 INTRODUCTION

Organisational environment is dynamic. Besides environmental changes there are changes in the job, their specifications, the technology used to execute them and the employees carrying out various organisational functions. The changes in the employees can be in the form of their movement within and outside the organisation. The movement of employees within the organisation can be in the form of transfer, promotion or job rotation. Transfer is movement of employees from one unit to another, the responsibilities and functions remaining the same. Promotion relates to vertical movement of employees in the hierarchy involving better status and increased responsibility. Job rotation is movement of the employee from one job to another to break the job monotory and to nable the employees to understand the total organisational system.

7.2 WHAT IS TRANSFER

Transfer is a lateral movement of employees from one position, division, department or unit to another. Such movement of employees from one job to another may be either due to promotion, demotion, organisational restructuring or may be for routine administrative reasons (some organisations do not allow employees to remain in the same job for a longer duration, which are sensitive in nature). Generally transfer does not involve any significant change in compensation, duties, responsibilities or even status.

7.2.1 Purpose of Transfer

1. To increase organisational effectiveness
2. To add to the versatility and competence of key personnel.
3. To cope with the fluctuations in work requirements.
4. To rectify erroneous placement.
5. To relieve boredom and monotony.
6. To set right incompatibilities in employees relations.
7. To look after the interests of the employees (their health or age-group, family problems etc.)
8. To provide creative opportunities.
9. To train employees for their future advancement or promotion.

7.2.2 Different Types of Transfer

1. *Production transfers:* Such transfers are done for stabilising employment. In an organisation, there may be several independent plants for different product-mix or shop-floors to produce sub-assemblies or components. Production in any of such plants or shop floors may get discontinued, either for dropping of the product or for other miscellaneous reasons. Such a situation necessitates production transfer.

2. *Replacement transfers:* Such transfers are effected during lay-offs, when senior employees may be transferred or relocated to protect their interest against employees with short service.

3. *Versatility transfers:* To prevent employees to develop proprietory interest in the job, materials and equipment used on the job and workloads, such transfers are effected, both for the benefits of the oranisation and the employees (employees gaining varied job experiences).

4. *Personal or Remedial transfers:* Such transfers are usually made in the interest of the employees, as employees often may request for transfer on grounds of health, age or family issues. To correct erroneous placement also such transfers are made.

5. *Shift transfers:* Such transfers are effected within the shift itself (without any change in job etc.), where shift system of work is prevalent. Shift system is a regularised rotation of employees from one shift to another.

7.2.3 Transfer Policy

In order to be impartial and objective, Transfer Policy and procedures must be established and make known to all employees.

A good transfer policy must answer the following questions:

1. What type of transfers are to be used? When?

2. What is the area over which transfers will be effected?

3. What is the basis used for effecting transfers?

4. Who is responsible for initiating and approving transfers?

5. Whether transfer should be permanent or a temporary one?

6. What is the rate of pay and other facilities the transferred employee should receive on his new job?

7. Whether training is necessary to effect a transfer?

However, in India, most of the organisations do not have well-formulated transfer policy, resulting to its gross misuse (often an instrument to victimise the employees). Public Sector Enterprises and Departmental Undertakings (Government Departments) often use this instrument without any regard to the cost aspect. Recently, Ordinance Factories Board had been adversely criticised for effecting meaningless transfer of officers and staff members, which involved crores of rupees of expenditure from public exchequer. For such irrational use, transfer related issues have now become important causal factors of industrial disputes in India.

7.2.4 Limitations of Transfer

Right of transferring abroad is not implied. However, in absence of provision in a contract of service to the contrary, a firm of Chartered Accountants with accounts in foreign countries may order an employee to go into a foreign state to work on a client's accounts. Many organisations, however, make it a point to include a paragraph in the terms and conditions of the letter of appointment of their would-be employee before its issue in a language or similar there to " You would be liable to transfer from your present place of posting to anywhere in India or abroad". This often saves the organisation from future confusion or embarrassment.

7.2.4A *New Branches*

When an employee is hired by a firm with no branches, there is no implied contract which permits his transfer to a branch thereafter established.

7.2.4B *Other Limitations of Transfer*

Although transfer, *per se*, is not punishment in the eye of law, transfers are limited by the standard of reasonableness. For example, although a bank can transfer its employees, it cannot harass them by doing so repeatedly. An order of transfer cannot be made which will result in a material change for the worse in the employee's contractual rights, such as reduction in his amenities like free quarters, medical assistance, fuel, electricity and cheap rations. Similarly, a radical change in the employee's duties may invalidate a transfer. And, in any event, an employee is entitled to reasonable time upon transfer to wind up his affairs.

At the end of this chapter, we have discussed the lateral transfer and horizontal transfer as promotion alternatives in detail.

7.3 PROMOTION

Promotion basically is a reward for efficiency. Promotion is conferment of additional benefits, usually in the form of higher pay, for an increase in responsibility or skill which is formalised by an increase in status or rank. Yet, in another way, promotion can be defined as advancement of an employee in an organisation to another job, which commands better pay/wages, better status/prestige and higher opportunities/ challenges and responsibilities, a better working environment, hours of work and facilities, etc. Thus, it has been observed that promotion is usually associated with the assignment of an individual to a position of more responsibility or to one which requires the application of his particular education or experience in a better way than now.

7.3.1 Promotion from Within

'Promotion from Within' as a system in an organisation outlines the policies and procedures for internal promotion of personnel. The basic difference between 'promotion' and 'promotion from within' lies in the fact that promotion policy in an organisation , as such, may incorporate provisions for recruitment from the outside to man promotional vacancies but 'promotion from within' policy in an organisation strictly provides for internal recruitment only to man such vacancies.

From the legal standpoint, however, no distinction, as such, is made between 'promotion' and 'promotion from within' and these two terms are interchangeably used.

7.3.2 Forms of Promotion

(a) *Informal and Formal:*

The two major forms of promotion are:

    i)   Informal promotion, and

    ii) Formal promotion.

The informal form of promotion or the promotion at the discretion of the employer is the oldest form of promotion, which enables the employer(s) concerned to promote those employees who have the requisite ability and merit.

The real problem of the informal form of promotion is that the senior managers may recommend for promotion only those individuals with whom they have already worked, or who, for one reason or the other, have impressed them by their activities or presence. This may sometimes result in promotion on the basis of prejudices of the employer and specialised knowledge and the abilities of the employees (which should form the basis of promotion) may be overlooked.

The formal form of promotion, contrarily, ensures objective evaluation of the responsibilities and duties vis-a-vis the different levels of an organisation. Significance of all the positions in the organisational structure is considered with a view of facilitating the objective appraisal of the capabilities of the individuals in the context of promotion. The formal form of promotion is also known as the standardised or systematic form. Seniority and length of service serve as the criteria to qualify for promotion under this form.

This form of promotion is strictly followed in the organisations having the 'promotion from within' policy.

(b) Open and Close:

Promotion may also be classified in a different manner,

(i)   Open form and

(ii)   Closed form.

In case of the open form of promotion, organisations do not restrict themselves to the existing employees only for the purpose of filling promotional vacancies. They announce such vacancies in order to harvest from the nation's 'personnel-crop' and to attract the best talents to the extent possible. But the closed form of 'promotion from within' policy, restricts the candidacy for filling promotional vacancies to the existing employees only of the organisation concerned.

(c) Other forms:

Again, promotion can be grouped according to the following four forms:

(i)   Movement to an authoritative position;

(ii)   Movement to a highly-skilled and highly-evaluated job;

(iii) In-grade progression (upgradation), and

(iv)   Widening of duties and responsibilities associated with the existing job with some increase in payment.

7.3.3 Elements of Promotion

We can deduce the following elements of promotion from the definition contents of promotion and promotion from within:

1. *Upward advancement* : Whatever may be the form of promotion, it necessarily implies upward advancement, i.e. movement of employees to higher positions in the organisational hierarchy. Although there are some promotions which, in reality, indicate upgradation or in-grade progression (i.e. promotion -in-situ), e.g. promotion of a clerk form Grade II to Grade I, strictly speaking, such promotions also imply upward advancement because the promoted

employees now occupy positions higher than their juniors in the organisation structure.

2. *Enhanced responsibilities, status and prestige:* Since change of job(s), consequent upon promotion, is quite common, the promoted employees are normally expected to assume higher responsibilities on being promoted. However, where promotion is somewhat in the nature of upgradation, the nature of the job being unchanged, responsibilities of the promoted employee mostly remain the same. In all other cases, enhanced responsibilities, status and prestige together constitute a basic element of promotion.

3. *Better pay and wages :* It is the next important element of promotion. But, promotion may not always entitle the promoted employees to higher emoluments, even though their responsibilities, status and prestige may enhance. In order to encourage creative behaviour in his functional area, an employee, whose contentment has almost reached a plateau, may be entrusted with a qualitatively different job which demands increased responsibilities and which enhances his status and prestige but not his emoluments.

4. *Other elements :* Better working environment, functional autonomy, scope for application of specialised knowledge, skill(s) and work experience, etc., are certain other important elements of promotion.

7.3.4 Purposes of Promotion

Promotion serves one important purpose of the employer, i.e., it enables him to adjust his workforce to the changing requirements. Moreover, from an employer's point of view, promotion is an important motivational tool as it can reduce employees' discontent and unrest.

Promotion can, therefore, improve the effectiveness of an organisation's structure in order to meet the targets and, at the same time, can considerably increase the effectiveness of its employees through assignment of suitable positions.

According to an expert in this field, the main purpose of promotion is to staff a vacancy that, in general, is worth more to the organisation than to the incumbent's present position.

In a more comprehensive manner, the purposes of promotion can be stated as follows:

1. To put an employee in a position where he will be of greater use to the organisation and where he is expected to derive increased personal satisfaction and have an increase in his emoluments;

2. To recognise an individual's performance and reward him for his work so that he may have an incentive to forge ahead;

3. To boost morale and encourage loyalty and help develop a sense of belongingness so far as an employee is concerned;

4. To promote job satisfaction and to motivate an employee to continue in the organisation;

5. To attract suitable and competent employees to the organisation and finally

6. To provide opportunities to an employee (who has not succeeded in gaining promotion) to enhance his skills and abilities required for superior performance.

It is important to note here that all the above mentioned purposes are equally served by the 'promotion from within' policy as well. That apart, the 'promotion from within' policy serves the following important purposes:

(i) It reduces employee-turnover and consequently reduces replacement cost;

(ii) It maintains high employee morale and productivity and finally

(iii) It maximises utilisation of human resources.

7.3.5 Promotion Policy

Promotional disputes in the recent years have become an important causal factor vis-a-vis industrial disputes in India (as these form an important part of the personnel related disputes and the disputes arising out of indiscipline and violence). Therefore, in order to avoid any possible complications in future and its consequential adverse effects on industrial relations, union-participation, as far as possible and so far as practicable, should be encouraged by management while formulating promotion policies.

7.3.6 Requirements of Promotion Policy

Some of the important requirements of an effective promotion policy are presented below:

(i) Preparing a statement showing ratios of internal promotions to direct recruitments at each level, mentioning the method(s) of selection (e.g., trade test and interview) and indicating the qualifications desired;

(ii) Identifying the network of the related jobs and the promotional channels for each job, taking into account the job relatedness, the opportunities for interacting with the executive placed in the higher levels with a view of fostering job learning and the qualifications (both academic and professional) and the work experience required;

(iii) Developing the procedural norms for determining employees' seniority and deciding upon whether it should be considered in a plant-wise or unit-wise or an occupation-wise manner and,

(iv) Developing the relationship between disciplinary action and promotions.

The Indian Institute of Personnel Management (now renamed as The National Institute of Personnel Management) has suggested that the following statements, etc., should be included in any standard promotion policy:

(i) A statement regarding promotion from within the organisation with a view to filling vacancies in higher posts;

(ii) A statement regarding the promotional bases like ability and seniority;

(iii) A well-drawn organisations chart in order to help all concerned understand the ladder of promotion; as well as the structural relationship of the employees working in the different positions among various professions functions and within their own profession/function.

(iv) A statement clearly mentioning the officials who may initiate and handle cases of promotion in order to help all concerned and

(v) A statement regarding provision for reversion in case a promotee's performance is not satisfactory.

7.3.7 Basis of Promotion

After formulation and acceptance by management of a sound promotion policy the next question that an organisation faces is 'What should be the basis for such promotions?' A decision in this regard is of utmost importance. In promotional decisions, the most important base is seniority. The Japanese concepts of Nenko Seido (i.e. promotion on the basis of age and length of service) and Shike Seido (i.e. statis remlomg), reflect nothing but seniority considerations in promotional decisions. In the USA and in the UK, seniority is an important factor of promotion. In India, seniority consideration in promotional decisions has not received much cognizance from organisations until recently. But, due to pressure from unions and subsequent changes in the government policies regarding promotional matters, seniority is fast emerging as an important consideration in the public sector. Different basis of promotion, however, are discussed as follows:

7.3.7A *Seniority*

Seniority refers to the relative length of service of employees. It may also be determined in relation to the age, occupation, department or organisation, of an employee. Basically, seniority implies skill formation through experiential learning. Seniority being quantifiable, provides an objective means of identifying the personnel eligible for promotion. Since biased managerial decisions on promotion can be averted to the fullest extent, seniority-criterion is widely accepted by employees. As promotion is predictable under the seniority system, it greatly reduces employee-turnover.

However, the seniority system has many disadvantages as well. Since merit or ability is altogether ignored, it does not guarantee quality staffing of promotional vacancies. Even though it is believed that, through experiential learning an individual develops his knowledge that aids in 'skill formation' during his long tenure of service, due to 'trained incapacity', he may be incapable of undertaking new assignments.

Moreover, what should be the basis of such seniority? Is it the total number of years of experience of the employee in the organisation plus the experience already gained in his past employments with other organisations or the experience (length of service) in the present organisation only? Should the experiences unrelated to the promotional vacant post be taken into account?

Mere consideration of seniority in the context of promotion, in reality discourages creativity and innovation. Despite the above demerits, the seniority-based promotion system is widely prevalent.

7.3.7B *Merit Rating*

The weaknesses of the seniority-based promotion system have resulted in developing the merit-based promotion system because that encourages excellence in an organisation. Merit is defined as efficiency and capacity of an individual judged in the light of his past performance. The obvious advantages of the merit-based promotion system are that it enhances organisational efficiency and maximises utilisation of talent (as only the deserving employees are promoted after thorough assessment of their abilities and performance). However, integrity of managerial personnel vis-a-vis determination of merit-criteria objectively is under suspect from the employees' side in general. And, that deters most of the organisations from using merit as the sole criterion in promotional decisions.

Even though the seniority-based promotion system is largely followed in the public sector organisations in India, the merit-cum-seniority approach plays a major role in promotional decisions in the private-sector organisations.

7.3.7C *Quota-system*

This system of promotion is mainly practised in government departments and public sector undertakings. The Government of India has framed rules/regulations regarding promotion of SC/ST employees who enjoy fixed quota. The organisations have to prepare and maintain Rosters for this purpose and whenever the turn comes, the existing SC/ST candidate has to be promoted without consideration of either seniority or merit.

7.3.7D *Trade Tests*

For staffing certain vacancies through promotion, specific trade tests are conducted in order to rate the candidates' trade-specific knowledge and skills. The ultimate promotional decisions are taken only after the candidates qualify in the specific trade test(s). For certain posts like fitter, turner, welder, etc. (technical) and stenographer, typist, etc. (non-technical), specific knowledge and skills are important pre-requisites. Thus, effecting promotion to these posts is subject to the candidates' ability to acquire such knowledge and skills. While some organisations stipulate minimum qualifying-service vis-a-vis one's eligibility to appear for such trade tests, most of the organisations usually allow their employees, irrespective of their length of service, to compete for such posts. In a strict sense, selection of an existing employee (after qualifying the stipulated trade test(s)) is not considered as promotion and can better be termed as reappointment (without break of service).

7.3.7E *Promotion by Examinations*

Examinations also play a major role in promotional decisions. Examinations, to a large extent, supplement the merit-rating system and provide opportunities to the talented employees for getting promoted to the higher posts without waiting for a long time. In some organisations, a minimum qualifying-service is stipulated vis-a-vis one's eligibility to appear for such examinations. In other organisations, qualifying in such examinations helps employees become eligible for promotion to certain posts. The Subordinate Accounts Services (SAS) Examination and Limited Departmental Section Officers' Examination for certain categories to the Central Government employees, the CAIIB Examination for the Bank employees, the Associateship Examination (conducted by the Institute of Actuaries) for the employees in the Insurance Companies, etc. are some examples for these types of examinations. However, the scope for promotion based on examinations is very limited because only a few departments of the Central Government and a handful of private organisations practise this.

7.3.7F *Age-group Preference*

In many organisations, a particular age group is preferred to other age-groups for staffing vacancies. The idea of preference for a particular age group is based on following considerations:

1.   Expected number of years of service;

2.   Possible source of supply of required manpower in future and

3.   Personality, dynamism, initiative, challenging attitude, etc.

Age is used as an index of stamina and flexibility and for determining the possible length of service before retirement. Although, no empirical support, as such, is available to relate promotion to preference for age group, many organisations, as a matter of policy, follow some norms regarding age groups vis-a-vis staffing of certain vacancies from within. In some cases, where the existing employees also contest with the outsiders for a particular vacancy, some relaxation in age is given to them. Thus, for the reasons stated earlier, preference for age group also influences promotional decisions.

7.3.7G *Personal Attributes*

Personal attributes like intelligence, health, energy, stamina, inherent attitude, interest and preferences, taken together, also form an important base for promotional decisions. Since these attributes are not quantifiable in the strict sense, rating by the superior is usually considered as a yardstick. More job experience, acquired knowledge and strong educational background may not make one competent or eligible for promotion. For example, certain jobs demand aptitude for figure work, which can only be found among those employees who have inherent interest in doing figure work. Similarly, poor health, lack of energy and stamina, etc. makes one unsuitable for sales jobs, supervisory jobs; require dealings with the public and leadership quality. Inherent attitudes, interests and preferences also, at the same time, act, in one way or the other, as important pre requisite for certain jobs. In many organisations, the system of writing annual confidential reports about employees exists. Certain columns in this report pertain to personal attributes. This report which is usually written by the superior concerned, thus, serves an important purpose of the management, i.e., considering the personal attributes of an employee for the purpose of taking promotional decisions.

7.3.7H *Performance Appraisal*

Performance Appraisal, in reality, is an important variable in promotional decisions. However, the term merit-rating is quite a narrow one and limited in approach. Performance appraisal has wider applicability in the context of evaluation of employees vis-a-vis their characteristics, qualifications, traits, capacities, proficiencies and abilities for the purpose of, inter alia, taking promotional decisions. Performances appraisal is basically a formal exercise in an organisation with a view to evaluating the employees' performance in a documented form at periodic intervals. A leading management theorist has identified the following three basic purposes of formal performance appraisal:

(i) To provide systematic judgements on salary increases, promotions, transfers, etc.;

(ii) To make an employee know 'where he stands' with respect to his boss; and

(iii) To provide a basis for coaching and counselling of an employee by his superior.

Although there are various methods of performance appraisal, the most widely-used method is Ranking. Under this method, ranking of an employee is done on the basis of comparison with others. An employee, who gets the highest numerical value to his credit (as compared to other employees), is considered most suitable for promotion.

Because of its simplicity and objectivity, the performance appraisal system is widely used throughout the world. An Indian study, covering 60 organisations, has indicated that companies, both in the public and private sectors, give considerable weightage (58 per cent) to performance appraisal for effecting promotional decisions.

7.3.8 Promotion Alternatives

'Promotion from within' as a regular process, apart from resulting in in-breeding, lack of dynamism and innovativeness, etc. has an inevitable danger of over-staffing of an organisation. Japanese organisations, which follow this system compulsrily even without 'objective assessment of employees' performance', have introduced an excellent promotion alternative, known as Status Ranking System, in order to obviate the problems of over-staffing. Under this system, a worker, who is otherwise eligible for promotion but cannot be promoted because of the problems of over-staffing. is awarded a Status Rank with increased allowance so as to make his pay almost at par with that of the promotable post. Thus, without actually promoting the eligible employees, this system ensures increased status for them in order to maintain their motivation levels and ensure their loyalty towards the organisation.

Inability to promote the eligible employees, for one reason or the other (e.g. the problem of over-staffing), is a problem of structural nature (because most of the employees have reached a plateau) before the management in any organisation. While job enrichment, job enlargement, lateral transfer, horizontal transfer, etc., which focus primarily on the change of work content, can in one way or the other, fulfil the intrinsic needs of the employees, these, in reality, reduce only the stresses resulting form content-plateauing. The problem of structure-plateauing remains unless suitable restructuring of the organisation, with due emphasis on reducing the importance of promotion and increasing the value of challenge, is attempted.

Since, temporary measures, job enrichment, job enlargement, lateral transfers and horizontal transfers can successfully reduce the stress of the employees, who are otherwise promotable, but are not promoted for the obvious inability of the organisations, these are considered as promotion alternatives. Ensuring timely promotion of employees is a major problem even for well organised and professionally-managed organisations in India. Government organisations, for the low-paid white-collar employees, relate their promotional decisions to the availability of vacancies, while, for the direct recruits in the officers' cadre, they have a system of promotion based on time-scale. This clearly indicates poor career planning, which results in serious motivational problems in the government organisations. Stagnation in different cadres for years together is a result of such ill-framed policy. Commercial banking organisations have made some progress in this matter, i.e. in the case of senior employees, the probability of getting promotion after completion of a certain number of years of service is quite high. But such types of measures are not at all adequate. However, job enrichment, job enlargement, lateral transfer and horizontal transfers can, to a large extent, alleviate the motivational problems of employees in such cases, at least, for the time being. Thus, an organisation gets an opportunity to restructure itself and can make some provisions for promotion during the intervening period.

7.3.9 Lateral Transfer and Horizontal Transfer

Two other promotion alternatives are lateral transfer and horizontal transfer. In the strict sense, transfer is the moving of an employee from one job to another. Such movement may either be horizontal or lateral. For internal mobility of the manpower, periodic transfers of employees are effected by an organisation either for the interests of the organisation or for the interests of the employee or for both. Although need for transfer may arise for one reason or the other (e.g. fluctuations in work requirements, increasing versatility and competence of key employees, correcting erroneous placements, relieving employees from monotony, protecting the interests of employees vis-a-vis their health or age and providing creative opportunities for employees), Indian organisations mostly relate transfer decisions to promotions, excepting cases where transfers of senior employees are affected for the maintenance of a tenure system. Since transfers, in most of the cases, involve change of place(s) and even, in some cases, result in reduction in material gains, transfer-decisions of an organisation, quite often, are resented by the affected employees. This is particularly evident in the Government and Commercial Banking Organisations. Problems of housing, education of children, inadequacy of compensation, disruption of family life and social life, etc. are some of the common grounds for which even promotional transfers are not accepted by many employees. In order to obviate such problems relating to implementation of transfer either for routine administrative reasons or for promotional reasons, transfer liability is usually made a pre-condition to employment. Most of the organisations have well drawn transfer policies in this regard. While, in other organisations, transfer is still a prerogative of the management.

Lateral transfer is the vertical movement of employees and denotes significant change in the work content. Cross-functional or cross-lateral tranfers, throughout the career of an employee, keep him fresh and receptive to new ideas and make him more creative and productive.

Horizontal transfer, on the other hand, is the movement within the same job-family. While job enrichment and job enlargement exercises do not involve, in reality, any movement from one job to another, lateral transfer and horizontal transfer indicate physical movement from one job to another and, thus, have some potential to motivate employees intrinsically.

Both lateral transfer and horizontal transfers can be effectively used for structure-plateaued and content-plateaued employees as temporary promotion alternatives. In some organisations, such transfers are made to equip the employees for assuming higher responsibilities consequent upon promotion.

7.4 JOB ROTATION

7.4.1 Job Mobility

Repetitive tasks develop boredom and jobs become increasingly dehumanised and dissatisfying to the employees. Some companies try to reduce this boredom through job rotation. Job rotation is a systematic movement of workers from one job to another. Such movement or rotation in different function increases the skills and functional efficiency of the employees as they are exposed to different business situations. Some companies even encourage such movement from one unit to another to enable employees to understand the organisation as a total system. For manning higher positions in the organisation, such knowledge of employees is an important pre-requisite. A staff executive, who is posted in an office, may be encouraged to move to the factory (which may not be attached to an office) to get exposed to the intricacies of life functioning, only to promote him later to a more senior position. Job rotation, for employees at lower level also, helps to multi-skill development whereby the organisation can get the advantage of their services at the time of exigency. However, frequent job rotations do not allow employees to get specialised knowledge and skill and reduce them to an unskilled functionary or at least 'a jack of all trades and master of none'. For such obvious disadvantage of job rotation, other forms of job mobility like, job enlargement and job enrichment are considered as better alternatives. These two forms have been discussed below.

7.4.2 Job Enrichment

Job enrichment is basically the restructuring of a job to make it more interesting and stimulating. This concept has been developed by Herzberg. Job enrichment seeks to improve task efficiency and human satisfaction and to provide greater scope for personal achievement and recognition, challenging assignment and opportunity for individual advancement and growth. Enough experimental supports, like the American Telephone and Telegraph Company Experiment and the ICI Experiment, have indicated that job enrichment has tremendous motivational potential and, if implemented properly, can significantly increase job satisfaction and productivity.

7.4.3 Job Enlargement

Job enlargement is the horizontal regrouping of tasks and implies mere additions of more functions and increase in the task variety. By enlarging job content, dehumanisation of work, as a result of excessive functional specialisation, can be reduced and the creative needs of employees can be satisfied to a large extent.

Even though job enrichment is a better alternative to job enlargement, as the former one is restructuring of a job in order to make it more interesting and stimulating and the latter is mere additions to a present job, both of these are considered important vis-a-vis satisfaction of intrinsic needs of the employees and fulfillment of their creative urges.

REVIEW QUESTIONS

1. Define Transfer. Why is transfer necessary for an organisation? What are the different types of transfer?

2. Is it necessary for an organisation to have a Transfer Policy? Justify your answer duly pointing out important components of a Transfer Policy? Do you think transfer is absolutely a management prerogative?

3. What is promotion? In what way does it differ from 'promotion from within'? What are the different forms of promotion?

4. Briefly state the elements and purposes of promotion.

5. You have been asked by an organisation to draft a promotion policy for their employees. What are the areas, you think you should consider, while drafting such a policy?

6. Briefly state the different basis of promotion. Identify at least three factors, which you think are important while taking a promotional decision.

7. Is it possible to ensure increased status for employees without actually promoting them? Select at least three promotion alternatives, which can confer increased status and job satisfaction to plateaued employees.

8. Write short notes on:

   a. Career Plateauing

   b. Standard Stroke Grade System

   c. Lateral Transfer

   d. Job Enlargement

   e. Job Enrichment

   f. Trade Tests

   g. Replacement Transfer

   h. Merit Rating

APPENDIX - I

Sample Promotion Policy in Commercial Banks

A Commercial Bank considers the following common factors in order to effectuate promotional decisions for the existing employees:

a. Seniority and /or length of service,

b. Professional qualifications,

c. Knowledge of practical banking,

d. Performance on the job and

e. Potential for development and growth.

However, weights assigned to each of the above factors vary from one bank to another and also depend on the levels of promotion. For each such factor, a maximum weight is assigned (stipulating certain conditions). The total score of each employee (applying for a higher post) is computed and the highest scorer is given the promotion. For example, for effecting promotion from the Junior Management Scale I post to the Middle Management (Lower) Scale II post, a maximum weightage for each of the above factors is fixed as follows:

a. Seniority and/or length of service - maximum weightage is 20 per cent (special extra weightage is given for those who are posted in the rural areas);

b. Professional qualifications - maximum weightage is 15 per cent

c. Knowledge of practical banking (evaluated through a process of written examination) - maximum weightage is 20 per cent

d. Performance on the job (assessed on the basis of evaluation of the performance of officers) - weightage varies from 10 per cent to 50 per cent depending on the ranks and

e. Potential for development and growth (assessed through a process of interview)- weightage varies from 15 per cent to 20 per cent.

Guidelines like these are followed in the case of effecting promotion from within for officers in the general stream. However, for officers in the specialists' stream like Law Officers, Engineers, Economists, Personnel Officers, etc. the policy of direct recruitment is followed.

For effecting promotion from the clerical cadre to the officers' cadre (Junior Management, Scale I), factors like service-seniority, educational attainments and performance in the written tests are given weightage.

For such promotion, commercial banks have introduced the following quotas for all the declared vacancies:

(i) 20 per cent of the declared vacancies are to be filled by the direct recruitment through the Banking Service Recruitment Board;

(ii) 50 per cent of the declared vacancies are to be filled on the basis of merit-cum-seniority from amongst the members of the clerical staff;

(iii). 30 per cent of the declared vacancies are to be filled on the basis of seniority from amongst the senior clerical staff (including the employees holding the special allowance posts).

Usually, the maximum age limit for promotion of the departmental candidates is fixed at 56 years both for promotion from the Junior Management Scale I post, to the Middle Management (Lower) Scale II post and promotion from the clerical cadre to the officers cadre (Junior Management, Scale I).

However, above promotion policy of commercial banks, is likely to get altered and changed, once Narasimham Committee Report of 1992 is implemented. The said report, inter alia suggested that individual banks should be free to make their own requirement, instead of present common recruitment system. The committee suggests that there is no need for setting up a Banking Service Commission for centralised recruitment of officers. This will provide scope for the banks to scout for talent and impart new skills to their personnel. The committee, however, predicts this recommendation on the assumption that the banks will set up objective, fair and impartial recruitment procedures and, wherever appropriate, they could voluntarily come together to have a joint recruitment system. As regards clerical grades, the present system of recruitment through Banking Service Recruitment Boards may continue but we could urge that the appointment of the Chairman of these Boards should be totally left to the coordinating Banks.

APPENDIX - II

Promotion Policy of Steel Authority of India (SAIL) Executives

Policy Objectives:

1. To man executive posts in the company with competent personnel having growth potential and to utilise their capability in working environment to the maximum through opportunities available for advancement.

2. To provide for a system which is conducive to equity, fairness and objectivity in matters concerning promotion of executives.

3. To ensure uniformity and consistency, to the extent possible in the promotions of executives of all units of the company.

4. To motivate executives of the organisation for better performance, by rewarding their contribution to the growth of the organisation, in deciding promotions on the basis of overall merit.

Scope

The policy shall cover all promotions made in executive posts (other than promotions from non-executive posts to executive posts) and shall apply to all units of Steel Authority of India Limited, for the purpose of promotion and career planning, all executives of SAIL will be classified as under:

Cadre	Grade Code
Jr Managerial	E-0 to E-3 (B)
Managerial	E-4, E-5
Sr Managerial	E-6(A), E-6(B) and E-7
Top Managerial	E-8

The executives will have to pass through all the standard scales without skipping any grade in accordance with this policy.

Minimum qualifications and eligibility criteria are different for different levels.

Promotion System

Vacancy Promotion System

This will apply in all grades except from E-1 to E-2. Subject to minimum requirements of promotion and fulfillments of criteria of promotion, the executives will be promoted to the next higher grade on availability of vacancies. Eligibility will be two years from (E-3(A) to E-3(B), E-6(A) to E-6(B), E-6(b) to E-7 and E-7 to E-8. In all other cases, it will be three years. Promotion from E-2 to E-3(B) will be through interview. Out of the candidates found suitable, promotion will be effected in order of seniority.

Standardised Strokes Grade System

Promotion from E-1 to E-2 would be on the basis of Appraisal Reports and qualifications as prescribed irrespective of vacancy. The eligibility for professionally qualified executives and Management Trainees (both technical and administrative) would be 4 1/2 years including the period of training of Management Trainees. For others, eligibility would be after completion of minimum 5 1/2 years service in E-1 grade. This selection will be subject to personal review/interview by the competent authority, from amongst those who have the prescribed appraisal rating. The prescribed appraisal rating will be three consecutive confidential reports being minimum C+ both under performance rating and printability rating.

Promotion from E-3(A) to E-3(B) would be on the basis of appraisal reports and qualifications only as prescribed, subject to completion of two years service in E-3(A). Individuals will get the monetary benefits, but not the designation which will be against the vacancy only.

Executives in E-6(A) will be eligible for promotion to E-6(B) provided they have put in two years service in the grade of E-6(A) on the basis of appraisal reports and qualifications only as prescribed. Individual will get the monetary benefits but not designation till a vacancy arises.

Criteria for Promotion

Following criteria for promotion would be followed:

> Appraisal Reports, as prescribed
>
> Qualifications, as prescribed
>
> Interviews, as prescribed
>
> Eligibility, as prescribed
>
> Discipline, viz., clearance for vigilance and disciplinary angle.

Minimum Educational Qualifications Required for Promotion within Executive Posts

Category of posts	Minimum Qualifications	Level
1. Technical	i) Matriculation with pre-selection training	E-0 to E-2 (upto and including)
	ii) B.Sc. or Diploma in Engineering	E-3(B) (upto)
	iii) Degree in Engg or equivalent	For E-4 and above
2. Non-technical	i) Bachelor's Degree	Upto E-3 (B)
	ii) Bachelor's Degree with professional qualification	E-4 and above

Contd....

3.	Mining	i)	Qualifications required under statute	Statutory posts
		ii)	Matric with pre-selection training	Upto and including the level of E-2
		iii)	Degree in Geology/Mining	Posts in E-3(B) and above
4.	Finance and Accounts	i)	Graduation with a pass in the departmental examination for Accounts or SAS Accountants Examination of the government	Upto and including the level of E-3 (B)
		ii)	Professional qualifications like CA/ICWA	Posts in E-4 and above
5.	Research and Development	i)	Degree in Engg or M.Sc. in related discipline	Upto and including the level of E-3 (B)
		ii)	Degree in Engineering preferably a Master's Degree or Doctor's Degree or Ph.D in Pure Science	Posts in E-4 and above

Schematic Representation of Promotion Systems

	System-A (Vacancy)	System-B (Standardised stroke Grade)	System-C (Service Linked Promotion)
1. Interview	Interview at job change level E-2 to E-3(A), E-3(B) to E-4, E-4 to E-5, E-5 to E-6(A), E-6(B) to E-7 and E-7 to E-8	Review/Interview	No Interview
2. Appraisal	last three appraisal with minimum 'C' and promotability rating	Appraisals with minimum 'C' and promotability rating.	Last three appraisals with minimum 'C' and performance rating
3. Qualification	As stated	As stated	As stated
4. Eligibility	Three years from E-2 to E-3(A), E-3(B) to E-4, E-4 to E-5, E-5 to E-6(A), E-6(B) to E-7 and E-7 to E-8	I. E-1 to E-2: 5½ years or 4½ years. II. E-3(A) to E-3(B): 2 years as E-3(A). III. E-6(A) to E-6(B): 2 years as E-6(A)	10 years
5. Discipline	Clear from vigilance and discipline angle	Clear from vigilance and disciplinary angle	Clear from vigilance and disciplinary angle

Note: Adopted from Personnel Policy Circulars of Indian Iron and Steel Company (a subsidiary of SAIL)

8 ATTITUDE MEASUREMENT

LEARNING OBJECTIVES

This chapter enables the reader to understand:

☐ employees opinions about their working environment through attitude survey.

☐ the role of HRD in attitudinal change.

☐ the various attitude scales used for measuring individual or group attitude.

CONTENT OUTLINE

8.1 INTRODUCTION

Attitude is a mental state of an individual which tends to act or respond or is ready to respond for or against objects, situation, etc., with which his/her vested feeling or affect, interest, liking desire and so on, are directly or indirectly linked or associated. During the course of development the person acquires tendencies to respond to objects. These learned cognitive mechanisms are called attitudes. Changes in knowledge are followed by change in attitudes. Attitudes are different from knowledge in a sense that attitudes are emotion-laden. Knowledge reinforces attitudes and re-inforced attitudes in the long run reinforces individual and group behaviour. Hence, attitude is neither behaviour nor cause of behaviour but it relates to an intervening pre-disposition or a frame of reference which influences the behaviour of an individual.

When the interest, feeling, etc. of an individual is not connected in any way with the object or situation, his/her responses (towards the said object or situation) will then not be attitude but opinion.

Attitudes or psychic state cannot be observed because psychological variables are dormant or latent. Being a covert, attitude measurement is difficult. Inference, prediction from behavioural data, interviews with structured questionnaires and scales are the usual tools for attitudinal measurement.

8.2 ATTITUDE SURVEY

To evaluate the human relation in the factories, industries and different organisations, attitude survey is indispensable. The study of attitude is also important in designing a training programme, which is a core HRD function.

Attitudes surveys focus on feelings and motives of the employees' opinions about their working environments. There are three basic purposes for conducting attitude surveys:

1. To compare results with other survey results,
2. To measure the effect of change that occurs and
3. To determine the nature and extent of employee feelings regarding specific organisational issues and the organisation in general.

Usually attitude surveys are carried out by interviewing a person with a structured close ended questionnaire. The skill of the interviewer is all important here for correct measurement of attitude. While framing the questionnaire, the interviewer should be cautious, as simple opinion – laden questionnaire items will not depict the attitude of the interviewee. What is important is to put value-laden questionnaire items, use of Behaviourally Anchored Statements, asking the respondents to rank any myth statements, etc. A sample list of such myth statements and value-laden questionnaire items is given below.

8.2.1 Myth Statements

1. Hard work ensures better result.
2. Linking to work with subordinates for prompt results.
3. Never say no to anyone; listen to everybody's problems.
4. One who is indispensable, is efficient.
5. Maintain the hierarchical structure while taking decisions, very rigidly.

8.2.2 Sample Questionnaire Items for Attitude Measurement

1. Do you think the expenditure on training is wasteful? (give your answer selecting any one from the given alternatives)

    a.   To a large extent

    b.   To some extent

    c.   To a very little extent

    d.   Not at all

2. What, to your knowledge, are the major barriers to effective implementation of flexible working hours in India? (Please arrange the factors in order of your perceived preference)

    a.   Lack of awareness

    b.   Difficulty in implementation

    c.   Supervisory problems

    d.   Lack of support from workers

    e.   Lack of support from unions

    f.   Production problems

    g.   Any other (please specify)

The first questionnaire item (which reflects the attitude of a person regarding training) can be evaluated by adding the weighted value of individual responses. How to give weight against questionnaire items has been explained in Scaling and Attitude Measurement part of this chapter.

Example:

Let the number of respondents be 15. Suppose they have given their responses as follows to the four alternatives:-

Alternatives	No. of respondents
(a) To a large extent	4
(b) To some extent	4
(c) To a very little extent	5
(d) Not at all	2
	15

Weighted average attitude:

Alternatives	No.	Weighted	Attitude
(a)	4	4	16
(b)	4	3	12
(c)	5	2	10
(d)	2	1	2

Alternative (a) 'To a large extent' is the group attitude.

The Second questionnaire item allows the respondents to answer the question by selecting all alternatives in order of their perceived priority. This requires use of factorial method for quantification of all responses. Let us give an example to illustrate the matter.

Example:

Let there be 15 respondents. Suppose they have responded by giving ranks to the alternative (a) as follows:

Respondent	1	2	3	4	5	6	7	
Rank of (a)	1	3	5	7	1	4	3	
Respondent	8	9	10	11	12	13	14	15
Rank of (a)	2	6	5	1	2	3	4	5

From the above, we get:

Priority/Rank	1	2	3	4	5	6	7
Number of respondents (Tr)	3	2	3	2	3	1	1

(Total no. of respondents = 15 No. of priorities/Ranks = 7)

Weighted Score Value is calculated as follows:

Priority	1	2	3	4	5	6	7
Total Value	3	2	3	2	3	1	1
Weights (factorial)	7	6	5	4	3	2	1
WSV	21	12	15	8	9	2	1

In the same way, the total weighted score value for other alternatives can be calculated from the responses obtained against each. Suppose they are as follows.

Alternative	b	c	d	e	f	g
Total WSV	65	30	70	55	60	40

The total weighted score value of alternative (a) is highest. Therefore, alternative (d) i.e., "lack of support from workers" should be the attitude/opinion of the group of respondents.

Similarly, sample Behaviourally Anchored Statements have also been given in previous chapters, as a tool to be used for Performance Appraisal.

For measurement of attitude, we can use various statistical tools. Since attitudes are psychological variables or qualitative variables, the first and foremost task for rater is to assign numerals to objects, events or persons. Use of Likert Type of Scale, Thurstone Scale, etc. help the interviewer to assign numbers, either discrete or continuous. Analysis of Variance, Corelation, Chi-Square Test, Kendal's Co-efficient and Concordance Test are some useful statistical tools for attitude measurement.

8.3 HRD AND ATTITUDINAL CHANGE

Changing attitudes, values and motivations are now the major issues before the organisations. Through appropriate HRD interventions, organisations can turn such changes into advantages, ensuring quality of work life, keeping pace with the changing human expectations. The following areas of attitudinal changes require HRD intervention:

a. Attitudes towards perceived threats to trade union legality and other large scale efforts to reduce trade union power or cohesion;

b. Attitudes towards methods of wage negotiations, whether by collective or local bargaining;

c. Attitudes towards working conditions and any administrative machinery for the discussion or regulation of such conditions;

d. Attitudes towards worker training or promotion and towards education in general as means of improving management and industrial skills.

As explained earlier, economic restructuring, market globalisation, international quality system standards, etc. have, inter alia, prompted the Indian organisations to go for radical organisation restructuring, which among others call for adoption of TQM principles in managing the human resources. TQM, inter alia, calls for Total Employee Involvement (TEI), Employee Empowerment, development of Small Group Activities (Quality Circle Forums), Value Engineering Teams, etc. To translate the TQM requirements into corporate practices, therefore, require lot of attitudinal changes at the top like; developing flatter type of organisation, de-layering delegation and informal organisational culture, where every employee need to be considered as a member of a well integrated family. To infuse attitudinal changes both at the top and at down the level, it is necessary to adopt following HRD strategy.

a. *Employee Empowerment:* Empowerment is to give everyone, instead just people with certain positions or certain job titles–the legitimate right to make judgements, form conclusions, reach decisions and then act. Empowerment, therefore, calls for employee participation in day-to-day problem solving and innovation. Traditional participative forums (Works Committee, Joint Consultative Machinery, etc.) restrict employee participation in operational areas. But empowerment demands employee participation in each and every corporate functions, so much so, as to accept the employee is not a mere seller of his time and labour for a contracted sum of money. The empowered employee acquires necessary skill and authority to make decision concerning quality and productivity. They initiate changes on their own. Empowerment changes attitude of the employee as it develops employee ownership and commitment.

b. *By promoting quality circles and developing the culture of total participation:* This has been discussed separately. However, this strategy is used to infuse attitudinal changes and to facilitate personal involvement of employees.

c. *By imparting knowledge and value-laden attitudinal changes in training:* Organisations need to focus on more Training on Human relations area like Leadership, Communication, Motivation, etc. Such knowledge inputs gradually reinforces the attitude of the employees.

d. *By focusing more on team spirit:* To integrate employees with the organisation. This initiative is further strengthened when we simultaneously ensure a sense of belongingness among the employees.

8.4 TYPES OF MEASUREMENTS

Type	Basic Empirical Operation	Typical Usage	Typical Statistics	
			Descriptive	Inferential
Nominal	Determination of equality	Classification of male-female, smoker, non-smoker, team-I, team-II, etc.	Percentage mode	Chi-square Binomial
Ordinal	Determination of greater or less	Rankings: Preference data, market position, attitude measurement many psychological measures, etc.	Median	Rank-order correlation
Interval	Determination of equality of Intervals	Index Numbers, Attitude measurement	Mean, Range, Standard Deviation	Product moment correlation T-Test, Factor Analysis
Ratio	Determination of equality of ratios	Sales, units produced, number of customers, costs, age, etc.	Geometric Mean	Coefficient of variation

8.4.1 Accuracy, Reliability and Validity

Accuracy is the extent to which a measurement is free from systematic and variable errors. Freedom from variable errors is known as the validity of measurement. Reliability measure yields same result in repeated applications to the same respondents or events. Validity measure is consistent as it is free from systematic error and measures what it purports to measure.

8.5 SCALES

Scale is an instrument with the help of which a concept is measured. It is used in all types of data collection techniques such as observation, interviews, projective techniques, etc. Broadly, there are two types of scales: Rating scales and Attitude scales.

8.5.1 Attitude Scales

Attitude scales measure one or more aspects of an individual's or group's attitude toward some object. Individual's responses to the various scales may be aggregated or summed to provide a single attitude for the individual. Similarly, group responses to the various scales may be aggregated or summed to provide a single attitude for the group.

These scales are of three types:

   a.   Likert's Summated Scales

   b.   Thurstone's Equal Appearing Intervals Scale and

   c.   Guttman's Cumulative Scale

8.5.1A *Likert's Summated Rating Scale*

A summated rating scale is a set of attitude statements of which all are considered or approximated as equal attitude value and to each of which subjects respond with degree of agreement or disagreement (intensity) carrying different scores. These scores are summed and averaged to yield an individual's attitude score. Under this method each respondent's ranking is found out by totalling his scores on all the statements (usually 5). To illustrate this let us have the following example:

S.No.	Statement	Agree	Disagree
1.	Advertising promotes sales	1	0
2.	HRD is exploitation of people	1	0
3.	Hard work increases productivity	1	0
4.	Effective time management reduces idle hours	1	0
5.	Money and other physical benefits are the only motivations	1	0

This procedure, however, suffers from following drawbacks:

   1. Ties in ranks occur quite frequently. There may be several respondents with total scores of 0, 1, 2, 3, 4, 5, who cannot be ordered in relation to one another.

   2. It does not throw light on the different ways in which given scores may be obtained. Different combinations of the score imply differences among individuals who are not revealed by this procedure.

   3. It is not possible to determine whether the scale is unidimensional or multidimensional, i.e. whether the statements are measuring only one property or several properties of an attitude.

   4. In this scale all statements are deemed to be of equal attitude value. There is no scale of statements as such. This method orders the individuals on the basis of their total scores and not statements.

Likert's Item Analysis

In this procedure respondents are asked to respond to a certain number of statements (which is usually restricted to 15). Reply to each statement is given in terms of five degrees of agreement or disagreement, viz., 'Strongly agree', 'Agree', 'Undecided', 'Disagree', 'Strongly Disagree'. Each statement, thus, becomes a scale in itself having five points on it. At one end of this scale is strong approval and at the other end is strong disapproval, between them there are many intermediate points. The respondent indicates with reference to each statement where he stands on this scale. The total of his scores on all statements is taken as the measurement of his attitude. Statement may be either favourable or unfavourable. For favourable statements, values given are 5,4,3,2,1, and for unfavourable statements values are 1, 2, 3, 4, 5.

The following example will illustrate this :

Statement	SA	A	U	D	SD
Management is a science	5	4	3	2	1
Management is not a science	1	2	3	4	5

8.5.1B *Thurstone's Equal Appearing Intervals Scale*

This scale attempts to represent the attitudes of a group on a specified issue in the form of frequency distribution. The various opinions or items on a scale are allocated to different positions in accordance with the attitudes they express. Following steps are necessary to construct a Thurstone Attitude Scale:

1. Brief statements expressing attitudes about a particular issue are gathered from current literatures or are especially prepared for this purpose. The statements should cover different range of attitudes from extremely favourable to extremely unfavourable and also include neutral statements.

2. Statements are given an arbitrary number for identification and a group of judges are asked to sort those into several piles.

3. After sorting, a complete tabulation is made to determine the number of times each statement is included in the several piles.

4. The scale values for each statement are determined graphically in the form of an ogive or cumulative frequency curve.

5. The final scale is then made, selecting 15 to 20 statements (preferably those on which judges have had least disagreement).

6. Respondents then are asked to check only those statements with which they agree.

The construction of this scale being very cumbersome and time consuming, it is usually avoided. Moreover, scale values assigned to statements are influenced by the attitudes, background and intelligence of judges who may see things different from the actual respondents. This scale also does not allow subjects to express the intensity of the feelings of the respondents as they have only the choice to indicate their agreement with the finally selected statements.

8.5.1C *Guttman's Cumulative Scale*

This scale is made up of a relatively small number of statements which have been tested for their unidimensionality. A unidimensional scale measures one variable only. The scale is known as cumulative as respondents agreeing with the most favourable statement are theoretically presumed to agree with all other statements expressing "lesser" degree of favourability. Use of this scale is also avoided for its complexity.

Other scale to measure the attitude is Social Distance Technique of Bogardus, which is normally used to measure highly subjective attitudes.

REVIEW QUESTIONS

1. Define Attitude. Why is the study of attitude necessary for HRD profession?

2. What are the different tools for attitudinal measurement? From an organisational point of view discuss in detail at least two measurement tools with due emphasis on their relative merits or demerits.

3. You have been retained by a company to study the attitude of their 50 employees on the recently introduced pension scheme. Develop at least 5 structured close-ended questionnaire, using Likert's Item Analysis Scale and interview the employees. Analyse all the responses using Factorial Method and measure the attitude of the employees.

4. Short notes:
    a. Equal Appearing Intervals Scale
    b. Cumulative Scale
    c. Summated Rating Scale
    d. Employee Empowerment and Attitudinal Change

9 ACCOUNTING AND AUDIT OF HUMAN RESOURCES

LEARNING OBJECTIVES

This chapter focuses on:

☐ process of human resource accounting and different approaches to the valuation of human resources.

☐ the objectives and importance of audit of HRD.

☐ the role of HRD auditor.

☐ HRD at national level.

☐ HRD at international level with special focus on HRD in Asian countries.

CONTENT OUTLINE

9.1 INTRODUCTION

A resource is defined as an object which can provide expected future services. Hence, objects which do not have expected future service potential, cannot by definition, be resources. People being capable of rendering future services, such potential services constitute a form of capital.

9.2 HUMAN RESOURCE ACCOUNTING (HRA)

HRA is the process of identifying, measuring and communicating data about human resources. Flamhoitz (1974) defined HRA as:

> *"Accounting for people as an organisational resource. It involves measuring the costs incurred by business firms and other organisations to recruit, select, hire, train and develop human assets. It also involves measuring the economic value of people to the organisation".*

HRA, therefore, shows how the organisation makes investment in its people and how the value of the people changes over time. Value of the employees increase by training (the core HRD activity) and experience over a time period. Such information on human resources facilitate effective management within an organisation.

9.3 VARIOUS METHODS OF VALUATING HUMAN RESOURCES

Different approaches to the valuation of human resources may be broadly grouped under two categories:

(a)   Non-monetary measurement

(b)   Monetary measurement

9.3.1 Non-monetary Measurement

Such methods involve the classification of human resources in terms of skills (skills inventory), performance evaluation, potentiality for development and promotion, attitude surveys and subjective value.

Skill is a coordinated series of actions to attain some goal. Operationally, skills are defined widely as overt responses and controlled stimulation. Overt responses may either be verbal, motor or perceptual. Verbal response typically stresses on speaking (which requires memorisation of words), Motor responses stress on movements of limbs and body while Perceptual responses stress on understanding of sensory responses. Controlled stimulation, on the other hand are energy inputs to the workers which we express in units of frequency, length, time and weight.

Basic concepts of rest of the method have already been introduced in relevant chapters, excepting the 'subjective value'. 'Subjective value method indicates a subjective evaluation of approximation of the likelihood of an event.

9.3.2 Monetary Measurement

There are number of monetary measurement techniques. Each such technique has its relative advantages and disadvantages. Here we will discuss such techniques very briefly, as under:

      1. *Capitalisation of historical costs method:* This method was developed by Likert. It capitalises all costs of recruitment, hiring, training and other

initial costs involved in developing a human resource, i.e. an employee. The amount so capitalised is written off over the period an employee remains with the organisation. If he leaves before the expected service period, the amount remaining as an asset is written off in its entirety in the year of leaving.

2. *Replacement Cost Method:* This method measures the cost to replace an organisation's existing human resource. It indicates what it would cost the concern to recruit, hire, train and develop human resources to match the present level of efficiency.

3. *Opportunity Cost Method:* Under this method, the value of human resources is determined on the basis of the value of an individual employee in an alternative use. If an employee can be hired easily externally, there is no opportunity cost for him.

4. *Economic Value Method:* Under this method human resources are valued on the basis of the contribution they are likely to make to the organisation during the period of their employment. The remuneration to be paid to an employee is estimated and discounted appropriately to arrive at the current estimated value.

5. *Present Value Method:* This method measures human resources; measuring by attributing employee's value to the organisation as an equivalent to the present value of his remaining earnings. Organisations like MMTC, ONGC, BHEL, ACC, Neyvell Lignite Corporation, etc. have already adopted this concept.

From HRD point of view, Human Resources Accounting helps to understand many pertinent issues like developing skill inventory, performance appraisal, assessing the individual's capacity for development, attitude surveys and subjective appraisal, as discussed above. Hence, for designing a Human Resource Information System (HRIS), we need to consider the following factors:

a. *Personnel Profile:* This includes name, sex, race, age, marital status, address and phone number service date, etc.

b. *Career Profile:* Performance appraisal, job title changes, job classification changes, salary changes, promotions, transfers, career paths, etc. are included in this profile.

c. *Skill Profile:* Education, training, certificates, licenses, degrees, skills, hobbies, requisite training, interests, etc. are combined in skill profile.

d. *Benefits Profile:* Insurance coverage, disability provisions, pension, profit sharing, vacation, holidays, sick leave, etc. are covered in the benefits profile.

9.4 HRD AUDIT

Personnel / Human Resources or HRD audit is a systematic survey and analysis of different HRD functions with a summarised statement of findings and recommendations for correction of deficiencies. Basically it examines and evaluates policies, procedures and practices to determine the effectiveness of HRD function in an organisation. HRD audit ensures that sound and cost effective policies are implemented. However, purposes and objectives of HRD audit can be listed as follows:

9.4.1 Objectives of HRD Audit

1. To determine the effectiveness of management programmes which facilitate management to develop, allocate and monitor human resources.

2. To analyse the factors involved in HRD and develop a statement of findings with recommendations for correcting deviations, if any, on following issues:

    a. The extent of deviation from HRD policies,

    b. To what extent objectives are spelt out,

    c. To what extent performance standards have been established.

3. To seek explanations and information and answers to all such above questions as: What happened? Why did it happen?

4. To study the extent to which line managers have complied with HRD policies and as such the operational problems in implementing the existing HRD policies.

5. To study the current manpower inventory and identify shortfall or excess, if any.

9.4.2 Job / Role of HRD Auditor

From the above stated objectives, the job of HRD Auditor can be enumerated as follows:

1. To get the current facts.

2. To study the effectiveness of the present system by answering following issues:

    a. Why was the practice introduced?

    b. What would be the result, if the practice is discontinued?

    c. What needs were intended to be fulfilled and have those been fulfilled or not?

    d. What could be the best possible alternatives for fulfilling such needs?

    e. What changes can improve effectiveness of existing practice?

    f. Are such intended changes economically and operationally viable?

    g. Are such changes sustainable from union's point of view?

    h. What should be the time frame for introducing the change?

9.4.3 Importance of HRD Audit

To keep pace with the changing environment, importance of periodic HRD audit has increased in recent years. Recent economic restructuring programme of the Government of India, as discussed earlier, prompted the need for restructuring of the organisation, which, inter alia, calls for restructuring of production, manpower, strategies, management practices and philosophies, etc. All such possible reasons for periodic HRD audit can be enumerated as follows:

    a. Technological changes, inter alia, are calling for renewal of knowledge and skills of existing manpower. Training function, therefore, has assumed importance. Periodic HRD audit can help to identify the changing training needs and development of new training modules for effective utilisation of manpower.

b. To keep pace with the environmental changes, management philosophy and practices at the organisational level also need to be changed, like Participative Management (through Quality Circles and Value Engineering Team), Employee Empowerment, Total Employee Involvement, etc. Need for all these can be understood only when we periodically undertake HRD audit.

Similarly, changing role of Trade Unions (which is now more pro-active than reactionary), Government (which is now more liberal than restrictive), emergence of new working class (who are more enlightened than their predecessors), emergence of international quality system requirements (which calls for scientific documentation of different corporate functions and infuse attitudinal changes), changing expectations of customers (which calls for more customer orientation), new statutory requirements (pollution control), etc., are now influencing HRD functions at the corporate level, effectiveness of which can only be understood by periodic HRD audit.

For all the reasons highlighted above, HRD audit has now become very important for organisations.

9.4.4 Scope of HRD Audit

For integration of personnel management with HRD functions, HRD audit now encompasses all the areas like review and integration of corporate mission, goals, policies and objectives, manpower planning, career planning and development, promotion and transfer policies, performance appraisal systems, training and development functions, recruitment and selection, etc.

9.4.5 Records Used for HRD Audit

Records provide ready reference and serve as future reference and guide. Reports, on the other hand, describe an incident, event or situation. Depending upon the organisation, the following records/reports are usually checked for HRD Audit. Time study records and time standards, cost records, records on scores obtained in tests and other examination, medical and accident reports, attitudinal survey reports, grievance reports, turnover reports, data on work stoppages, performance reports, pay roll data, labour costs data, etc.

9.4.6 Methods and Techniques of HRD Audit

HRD audit can be carried out either by attitudinal survey or by interpreting data. Details of attitudinal survey have already been explained in a separate chapter. Interpretation of data can be done either by simple comparison over a period or by ratio analysis or by graphical or pictorial displays. The following examples illustrate the data interpretation method.

9.4.7 Checklists for HRD Audit

T.V. Rao and Udai Pareek (1996), to measure the effectiveness of people management developed a set of 20 questions mostly to suggest linking of HRD to the corporate objectives, goals and strategies, effectiveness of free flow of HRD information down the ranks, application of knowledge of behavioural science and industrial psychology for HRD, etc.

For other HRD sub-systems too, they have developed similar sets of questionnaires, adding responses which can help an organisation to audit their HRD activities. However, using same general checklists for all organisations may not be very effective to audit human resources for its obvious uniqueness in functions, practices and philosophies.

9.5 PERSONNEL RESEARCH

Information on personnel can be made available in two forms; the first one includes facts, terms and concepts or ideas, while the second one is in the form of predictions and explanations. The second form is the product of research. Personnel Research is the detailed analytic study about people of the organisation by conducting attitudinal survey or direct interview with structured, close ended questionnaire. By simple analysis of data also research can be carried out, but that may not give much insights on employees' attitude or intrinsic feelings.

There are different phases of Personnel Research like, fact finding, hypothesis formulation, valuation and interpretation and application of the results, etc. In India, many organisations carry out systematic personnel research. However, systematic personnel research can help organisations to combine people and procedures, study pattern of supervisory behaviour, supervisory skills, identify need for changing policies and procedures, etc.

9.6 HRD AND NATIONAL PLANNING

Importance and imperativeness of HRD at the orgnisational level has already been highlighted in our introductory submission. At the national level also, focus on HRD activities is absolutely necessary to develop employable human resources. Development of employable human resources is possible once we go for developing infrastructural support for increasing the literacy, developing graduates and post-graduates, professionals, scientists, etc. whose knowledge could be utilised in the organisations. Realising this importance, Government of India has now even set up a Human Resource Development Ministry. However, at the national level, HRD does not mean only education and training. It as well encompasses health, housing, provision for drinking water, hospital and medical facilities, social security and other welfare measures, etc. Even though budgetary allocation for HRD in India is not upto the mark, the trend indicates HRD has started receiving priority like any other national issues in National Planning. A comparative analysis of Human Development Data indicates that availability of employable people is relatively less in India, even though population growth is much on the higher side. By the employable or employability, it is meant that availability or adequate human resources with high technological literacy and managerial competencies. Realising this importance, recently World Bank has sanctioned aid for Rs 1, 650 crores to India for revamping and upgradation of our education system, covering 539 Polytechnics in 17 states and 2 union territories. As on date, we are having 300 recognised technical education institutes at the degree level and 750 polytechnics at the diploma with annual admission capacity of 65,000 and 90,000 students respectively. Besides this, facilities for post graduate studies and research work benefit another 11,000 scholars.

Many organisations in India have of late started taking active interest in developing human resources collaborating with Technical and Management Institutes.

The Table 9.6.1 below indicates, resultant human development efforts of Government of India vis-a-vis comparison of such data with other Asian countries.

9.6.1 Human Development Indicators for Some Asian Countries -1992

Countries	Literacy Rate (per cent)	Life Expectancy	Infant mortality (per '000)
China	80	70.5	27
Indonesia	84.4	62.0	66
India	52.2	60.8	74
Malaysia	80.0	70.4	14
Philippines	90.4	64.6	40
Pakistan	36.4	58.3	99
Republic of Korea	96.8	70.4	21
Singapore	92.0	74.2	08
Sri Lanka	89.1	71.2	24
Thailand	93.8	68.7	26

Source: Economic Survey, 1994-95, Government of India, Ministry of Finance, Economic Division

The Table 9.6.1 above indicates , how poor is India's human development data in comparison with many other Asian countries. The expenditure of India on human development in comparison with other Asian countries (listed above), as presented in Table below, further indicates that India is spending comparatively very less percentage of her GDP, though the emphasis indicates a minor trend of growth.

9.6.2 Selected Expenditure by Categories As Percentage of GDP for the Year 1981 to 1985 and 1986 to 1991

Countries	Social Security	Education	Health	Housing and Community Amentities
China	0.4 (0.3)	3.8 (3.6)	... (...)	... (...)
Indonesia	.... (...)	1.1 (1.0)	0.5 (0.4)	1.2 (1.1)
India	.... (...)	0.3 (0.4)	0.3 (0.3)	0.7 (1.1)
Malaysia	1.9 (2.0)	5.8 (5.8)	1.5 (1.5)	1.6 (0.3)
Philippines	0.3 (0.2)	1.9 (2.7)	0.6 (0.7)	0.4 (0.1)
Pakistan	1.1 (...)	0.6 (...)	0.2 (...)	0.7 (...)
Korea	1.1 (0.7)	3.3 (3.0)	0.3 (3.0)	1.1 (1.3)
Singapore	2.9 (0.7)	4.1 (4.8)	1.2 (1.2)	1.4 (3.2)
Sri Lanka	0.7 (3.7)	2.4 (2.7)	1.3 (1.6)	0.3 (0.4)
Thailand	5.5 (4.6)	3.9 (3.1)	1.0 (1.0)	0.4 (0.3)

Source : Asian Development outlook, 1994, Asian Development Bank, Oxford University Press, Hong Kong, 1994.
Notes: Figures in parenthesis indicate data for the year 1986-91
For India, figures in parenthesis are for the year 1986-89

This therefore, suggests shifting of priority for Indian Planners for developing human resources.

9.7 HRD FROM WORLD PERSPECTIVE

In New Delhi, during 19-23 January, 1995, Labour Ministers of Non-aligned and other developing countries met to debate on human resources. In the said meet, Labour Ministers took stock of the current world economic scenario vis-a-vis its impact on human resources in developing countries. The meet emphasised:

1. The need for effective workers participation for enhancing productivity.

2. The need for adopting employment policy in congruence with the national economic and social development policy.

3. The need for education and training of workers and building economically valuable stock of technicians, scientists, technologists and management specialists by increasing access to education, making it equitable and affordable.

4. Need for vocational guidance and counselling.

5. Need for promotion of self employment.

6. Need for striking a balance between labour protection through state intervention and market flexibility.

7. Need for eliminating gender discrimination and enhance participation of women in all economic activities.

8. Need for elimination of child labour.

9. Need for safeguarding the interest of international migrant workers.

10. Need for establishing internal labour standards.

Regarding human resources and skill development the meet reached to a consensus and adopted following resolutions:

a. To establish policies and practices to secure investment of requisite proportion of the Gross National Income as government expenditure in education and training.

b. To study sub-sectoral priorities (between primary, secondary and tertiary levels of education) and analyse investment ratios between the sub-sectors and maximise the rate of return on investment.

c. To enhance access to and retention in education and training and thereby avert wastage of educational investments.

9.7.1 HRD in Asian Countries

Indonesia

In Indonesia, change in employment relationship for technology and consequent restructuring of the organisation is controlled by the Government for obvious surplus of labour in the labour market. The employment matters being highly regulated in Indonesia, scope of organisation-wide HRD activities is limited.

Malayasia

Malayasian economy is now facing extreme recession. Termination and lay-offs are very frequent in industries, which obviously restrict the HRD activities.

Philippines

Philippines Industries are facing the challenge of new technology, which resulted in large scale displacement of workers, skills-mismatch and redundancy. This situation is being settled by wide spread training and development programmes in the industries.

Singapore

Singapore has established Skills Development Fund to counter the effect of technology and train the workers.

Thailand

The extent of HRD activities in Thailand are limited. Retraining efforts to help the workers to make them adaptable to changes are also not that adequate.

REVIEW QUESTIONS

1. Define Human Resource Accounting. What are the different methods of Human Resource Accounting?
2. For designing Human Resource Information System, what are the factors that need to be considered?
3. Define HRD Audit. What are its objectives and importance?
4. What should be the role of an HRD Auditor?
5. What is the scope of HRD audit? What records need to be used for it?
6. Briefly explain methods and techniques of HRD audit.
7. What is the significance of HRD for National Planning?
8. Short Notes:
   (a) Personnel Research
   (b) Human Development Indices
   (c) Technology and HRD
   (d) Checklist for HRD audit
   (e) Career Profile
   (f) Present Value Method

10 WAGES AND SALARY ADMINISTRATION

LEARNING OBJECTIVES

This chapter illustrates:

- ☐ importance and objectives of wage policies
- ☐ basis of wage determination
- ☐ concepts of job evaluation, job design and job description
- ☐ types of job evaluation schemes
- ☐ various steps in Time Study
- ☐ various Incentive schemes.
- ☐ definition and importance of Fringe Benefits

CONTENT OUTLINE

10.1 INTRODUCTION

In constructing a wage structure in a given case industrial adjudication does take into account to some extent considerations of right and wrong, propriety and impropriety, fairness and unfairness. As the social conscience of the general community becomes more alive and active, as the welfare policy of the state takes a more dynamic form, as the national economy progresses from stage to stage, as under the growing strength of the trade union movement collective bargaining enters the field, wage structure ceases to be a purely mathematical problem. Considerations of the financial position of the employer and state of national economy have their say and the requirements of a workman living in a civilised and progressive society also come to be recognised, it is in that sense and no doubt to a limited extent, that the social philosophy of the age supplies the background for the decision of industrial disputes as to wage structure.

It is against these backgrounds that the framers of the constitution incorporated in Article 43 of the Constitution as part of the Directive Principles of State Policy that, *"The State shall endeavour to secure, by suitable legislation or economic organisation or in any other way, to all workers - agriculture, industrial or otherwise - work, a living wage, conditions of work ensuring a decent standard of life and full employment of leisure and social and cultural opportunities".* By this declaration the State not only bound itself to the importance of the State's role in directly promoting welfare, it recognised the inadequacy of the market forces to determine a wage level which is consistent with any welfare standards of a living wage. The declaration, in effect, gave assurance to labour that where they were not able to secure for themselves a living wage, the Government through legislation or other means will come to their aid. Two aspects of the State's role vis-a-vis the workers can be seen here, one, use of the State's authority to prevent employers from taking undue advantage of the workers weak bargaining strength and two, direct participation of the State on the economic life of the nation through planning and expansion of the public sector. The former was meant to give the worker a fair share in the kitty and the latter to enlarge the kitty itself.

10.2 WAGE POLICY

The recommendations of the Committee on fair wages, 1948, provided the basic approach for tribunals, Wage Board and others to fix wages of workers, a large part of which has been accepted by the Supreme Court in the case of Express Newspapers (Pvt) Limited and others Vs. The Union of India, 1938. Broadly speaking wages have been classified into (1) Minimum Wages, (2) Fair Wages and (3) Living Wages.

There is under any set of economic circumstances a minimum that a worker must have. This minimum is 'need based' and represents a level of wages which are just adequate to satisfy the minimum human needs of worker and his family. The notion of 'minimum wage' implies that irrespective of any other consideration a worker must receive this wage. If any industry is not in a position to pay even this level of wages then, it is clear that non-labour resources are being utilised inefficiently and should better be utilised in a different channel.

Accordingly, the resolutions adopted at the 15th Indian Labour Conference, 1957, with regard to minimum wage are as under:

1. In calculating the minimum wage the standard working cost per family should be taken to consist of three consumption units for one earner. The earnings of women and children and adolescents should be disregarded.

2. Minimum food requirement should be calculated on the basis of a net intake of 2700 calories as recommended by Dr Aykroyd (Dr Aykroyd's Health Bulletin No. 23) for average Indian adult of moderate activity.

3. Clothing requirement should be estimated at per capita consumption of 18 yards per annum which would give for the average workers' family of four, a total of 72 yards.

4. In respect of housing, the norms should be minimum rent charged by the government in any area for house provided under the subsidised scheme for low income groups.

5. Fuel, lighting and other miscellaneous items of expenditure should constitute 20 per cent of the total minimum wages.

Even these needs just as any other set of needs cannot be described as the 'minimum' for all the different groups and categories, for they are flexible and relative in respect to time, place, class, etc. Realising the difficulty in applying them to real life situations, no tribunal or wage board has made any attempt to quantitatively define the minimum needs precisely while fixing workers' wages although, every tribunal wage board has made a passing reference to those recommendations.

The concept of fair wages involves a rate sufficiently high to enable the worker to provide a standard family with food, shelter, clothing, medical care and education of children appropriate to his status in life but not at a rate exceeding the wage earning capacity of the class of establishment concerned. A fair wage, thus, is related to a fair work load and the earning capacity.

The living wage concept is one or more steps higher than fair wage. According to Mr Justice Higgins, the living wage must provide not merely for absolute essentials such as food, shelter and clothing, but for condition of frugal comfort estimated by current human standards including provisions for evil days, etc. with due regard for the special skill of the workman. Fair wage lies between the concept of minimum wage and the concept of living wage.

While the lower limit of the fair wage must obviously be the minimum wage, the upper limit is equally set by what may broadly be called the capacity of industry to pay. This will depend not only on the present economic position of the industry but on its future prospects also. Between these two limits the actual wages will depend on the productivity of labour, the prevailing rates of wages in the same or similar occupations in the same or neighbouring localities, the level of the national income and its distribution, the place of the industry in the economy of the country.

Confining within the boundaries of the fair wage concept, every industry must also strive to ensure fair growth in the remuneration to its workmen. First of all the current purchasing power of workers should be maintained against price rise by providing for adequate neutralisation in respect of the rise in the cost of living so that there is no erosion in their total emoluments in terms of their purchasing power. The workers resist any attempts in direct and visible cut in their wages. But in case of indirect cuts in their wages in the form of erosion, they suffer in silence and in misery. This despair on the part of workers leads to low morale, etc., which in turn results in low efficiency and productivity.

Secondly, a reasonable growth in the real earnings of workers should be aimed at improving their living standards, commensurate with their level of productivity, firms' profitability and other factors.

10.2.1 Objectives of Sound Wage Policy

The following are the objectives of an ideal wage and salary policy:

(i)   To establish good labour relations.

(ii)   To decide on appropriate wages.

(iii)   To decide wages based on individual's capability.

(iv)   To develop a pre-determined scheme for payment of wages.

(v)   To establish linkages of wage payment with performances.

(vi)   To maintain parity of wages with other organisations.

(vii)   To provide for incentive payment.

(viii)   To guarantee minimum wages.

(ix)   To provide for neutralisation of price rise.

(x)   To develop wage structure which can attract the talent.

10.3 WAGE DETERMINATION

Wage determination involves job evaluation, job design, job assessment, job analysis and job description.

10.3.1 Job Evaluation

Job Evaluation originated in the United States in 1971. In 1909, Civil Service Commission in Chicago and the Commonwealth Edison Company of Chicago pioneered the field. In 1926, Merill R. Lott wrote a book on 'Wage Scales and Job Evaluation', describing methods used in his company, the Sperry Gyroscope Co., Inc.

It is the process of determining the worth of one job in relation to that of another without regard to the personalities. It analyses and assesses the content of jobs, to place them in some standard rank order. The end result is used as the basis for a fair and logical remuneration system.

A properly devised job evaluation scheme provides management with definite, systematic and reliable data for working out wage and salary scales. Thus, logical wage negotiation reduces wage grievances and dissatisfaction with wage differentials and ensures fair treatment for each employee. It also provides a logical basis for promotion. A survey of British Institute of Management indicated following reasons for its use:

1.   To reduce layout turnover,

2.   To increase output,

3.   To improve morale,

4.   To reduce loss of time due to wage negotiation and disputes,

5.   To reduce the complaints regarding wages,

6.   To reduce wage and salary anomalies.

10.3.1A *Steps in Job Evaluation*

1.   Through examination of the Job (Job Assessment),

2.   Preparation of Job Description (recording its characteristics to suit assessment of method),

3   Preparation of Job Analysis to set out the requirements of the job under various factor headings,

4.   Comparison of one job with another,

5.   Arrangement of jobs in a progression,

6.   Relating the progression of jobs to a money scale.

10.3.1B *Types of Job Evaluation Schemes*

There are four basic types of Job Evaluation, which can be enumerated as follows:

1.   *Ranking:* This is a simple system to judge each job as a whole to understand its relative worth by ranking one whole job against another job. To start with, a job description is prepared in a narrative form, starting duties, responsibilities and qualifications, required for the job. Jobs are then ranked in order of relative difficulty or value to the company and grade levels are then defined and wage levels are finalised. One of the disadvantages, this method has that the degree of difference between jobs cannot be indicated. Ranking, therefore, may be incorrect and unduly influenced. Relative value of the employees (currently occupying the jobs) may be ranked rather than the jobs. The methods may be adequate for the easily defined jobs of a small number of workmen but it is regarded as impracticable for complicated jobs and large number of workmen.

2.   *Classification:* This is different from ranking as in this case grade and wage levels are pre-determined before jobs are ranked and descriptions are written defining the type of job which should fall into each group. Under this method, usually a committee allocates jobs to each group using job description. The system is simple but suffers from limitation similar to that of Ranking System.

3.   *Points rating*: Under this system, to achieve a higher level of accuracy, each job is broken down into its component factors or characteristics and then evaluated separately rather than evaluating the job as a whole. A narrative job description is prepared and supplemented by a statement of the various requirements (present in the job). Characteristics like experience and training, mental and physical effort, common to the jobs are selected and a point value for each characteristic or factor is determined. Factors are defined objectively and points are given to each factor based on its estimated importance. Consolidated point values are finally converted into money terms.

4.   *Factor comparison:* This method is also similar to the Points Rating System as here also each job is broken into factors. The only difference, here five factors are used, i.e. mental requirements, skill requirements, physical requirements, responsibility and working conditions. After job descriptions, key jobs are judged and related to one another. The jobs are considered one by one and reviewed to understand how much of the current wage rate for the job is paid for each factor. Key jobs are arranged in a scale in order of their value for each factor.

Remaining jobs are compared with the key job factors and a comparative money value is determined for each factor in each individual job. The total of the factor values so determined for each job represents its rate. This is a complex system, however, higher degree of accuracy can be attained through this.

10.3.1C *Limitations of Job Evaluation*

Job evaluation alone cannot establish a wage scale. For wage fixation, we need to take into cognizance statutory requirements, like Minimum Wages Act, 1948. Similarly, other factors of wage fixation like, capacity to pay, inter-industry wage variation, inter-regional wage variation, collective bargaining agreement, if any, also need to be given importance. Job evaluation is highly subjective (being based on judgemental estimate). Similarly, it cannot take into account the cyclical effect of market value on occupations. For example, finance jobs were highly priced in the market at one point of time (now IT and Marketing has taken its place). However, with the failure on NBFC, finance jobs are not that highly priced in the market at least at this point of time, even though no material change in the job profile of finance professionals have taken place in between.

Despite such limitations, job evaluation technique is considered very useful for reasons explained earlier.

10.3.2 Job Design

Every work undergoes constant modification because of the impact of mechanisation and automation. Some jobs become redundant while others are created and still others are altered in content. This necessitates different types of education, experience and other attributes. Also for effecting Job Design, the organisation needs to respect the unions, who otherwise may stall the move on one ground or the other.

While designing a job, management must also be concerned with the practical considerations of quantity and quality of available personnel (both within the organisation and in the labour market). Personality conflict and friction, problem of human relations, boredom, obsessive thinking, etc. also need to be taken care of.

Thus the factors, which are likely to affect job design can be enumerated as follows:

1. Job specialisation and repetitive operations,
2. Changing technology ,
3. Labour-union policies,
4. Abilities of present personnel ,
5. Adequate availability of potential personnel,
6. Interaction among jobs with the system and
7. Psychological and social needs that can be met by the job.

10.3.3 Job Assessment

At this stage information about each job is made available to the assessors. Every job, whether manual or not, is closely observed and inspected in actual operation by the assessors. If required, assessors question the operators and their supervisors to collect further details about the job to clear doubts if any. To keep pace with the changing job content, due to technological changes, it is necessary to make periodic re-assessment of the job keeping in view the old job description.

10.3.4 Job Analysis

This process helps to examine the facts about some specific job and determine the essential job factors. Therefore, the exercise helps to identify the qualities like skill, training experience, etc. required of the worker to perform his jobs satisfactorily. The analysis is primarily based on Job Description Sheet. However, to supplement the analysis further details may be obtained from personal observation and discussion.

10.3.5 Job Description

This process helps to give a title to a job, considering the conditions, tasks and responsibilities involved and qualities required for a job. Even though, the terms 'Job Description' and 'Job Specification' are used interchangably, there is a distinction, like; job description process defines the job content, i.e. the conditions, tasks and responsibilities, while job specification denotes the job requirements, i.e. the qualities that are necessary in a worker, to satisfy the demands of the job. Qualities may be either physical or mental attributes or the both.

While describing a job, it is necessary to record following details:

1. Purpose of the tasks, i.e. the end-result,
2. Frequency of recurrence of the tasks,
3. Accuracy limit,
4. Environment and conditions under which the job has to be done,
5. The tools and equipments that are required to perform the job,
6. Coordination and contacts with others required to perform the job,
7. Nature and amount of supervision and instruction required for the job,
8. Type and nature of specialised skills and knowledge required to perform the job,
9. Responsibilities involved in the job,
10. Origin of the job and its end-use, etc.

After recording the above details and its analysis, job-titles are given to designate various occupations. While designating occupations, it may be required to consider a specific job, like the job of a carpenter or the job as a whole like a Systems Executive. Some jobs may be classified or described under some common job-families, where instead of giving any specific title to a job, it is the usual practice to define various grades, like highly-skilled, skilled, semi-skilled or un-skilled. Combining jobs in common job-families is done considering the job proximity, like job of a Book keeper, Accounts Assistant, Cashier, may be grouped under one common job-family, i.e. Clerk.

In the determination of wage differentials and wage structure, job evaluation as a tool has to be thought of with adequate caution. Other techniques, discussed above also to a great extent influences the wage determination process.

10.4 WAGE BOARDS

Wage Boards consist of an impartial Chairman, two other independent members and two or three representatives of workers and employers each. The recommendations of the board are first submitted to the government for its acceptance. After acceptance, the government requests the parties to implement them.

The board is required to take the following points in determining the wage structure-

    a.   Need-based minimum wage,

    b.   Industry's capacity to pay,

    c.   Productivity of labour,

    d.   Prevailing rates of wages,

    e.   Level of national income and its distribution,

    f.   Place of industry in the economy of the country;

    g.   Need of its development,

    h.   Requirements of social justice,

    i.   Adjustment of wage differentials in such a manner as to provide incentives for skill formation.

Collective bargaining is also another important method of wage determination and is very successful in industries. We have discussed this technique in detail in a separate chapter.

10.5 TIME STUDY

Time Study technique is also used for wage determination. We have briefly introduced the concept here and then illustrated the method suitably designing a problem.

ILO defined Time Study as "a technique for determining as accurately as possible from a limited number of observations the time necessary to carry out a given activity at a defined standard of performance". For carrying out a time study, equipments like stopwatch, study board, pencils, sliderule, etc. are required. The stopwatches are of different types like–

    1. Stopwatch which records one minute per revolution by intervals 1/5th of a second with a small hand recording 30 minutes;

    2. Stopwatch which records one minute per revolution, calibrated in 1/100th of a minute with a small hand recording 30 minutes;

    3. Decimal-hour stopwatch recording 1/100th of an hour per revolution graduated in 1/1000th of an hour and a small hand records upto one hour in 100 divisions.

10.5.1 Steps in Time Study

Following steps are necessary for carrying out a time study for measurement of work:

    1. To collect and complete all available information about the job, which should also include surrounding conditions and so also the attributes of the operators, which are likely to affect the work.

2. To record the details of the method and also to break down different operations into elements.

3. To record the time taken by the operators to perform the operation (element-wise) measuring preferably with a timing device like stopwatch.

4. To assess the working speed of the operators comparing the same with a predetermined normal speed.

5. To convert the observed time to normal time.

6. To decide the rate of allowances which may be given over and above the normal time of the operation.

7. To determine the allowed time for operation.

10.5.2 Problems on Time Study

Time study is a work measurement technique, which is widely undertaken in industry to decide the standard time and then to compare the time taken by the workmen. Though, it basically helps in pricing a job, it is also used for other purpose like deciding on training requirements, payment of incentives and rewards, etc. Let us try the problem below to understand its computational details.

10.5.2A *Problem*

You have been asked to set the standard time for manufacturing ball point pens based on the following activity details. You have observed the ongoing job for 100 hours and have seen that within this period 1000 ball point pens have been manufactured. Assume that during work, workmen get personal time allowance @ 10 per cent. Compute Standard Time for manufacturing a single ball point pen.

Activity	Rate (per cent)	No. of times jobs observed
A	120	200
B	90	300
C	80	500
D	70	100
Idle Time		200
Total observed Time =		1300

Solution

To solve this problem, at the outset, it is necessary to compute Average Cycle Time, dividing observed period by number of ball point pens produced;

i.e. 100 hours / 1000 ball point pens = 1/10 of an hour, i.e, 6 minutes.

Thus, 6 minutes on an average is taken for manufacturing a ball point pen.

Now we have to compute activity-wise distribution of time using this formula:

Average Cycle Time x (Observed Time/Total Time) x Rating

Average Cycle Time has already been computed, which is 6 minutes.

Observed Time is the activity-specific time, already shown in the problem.

Total time is total observed time. Rating is the perceived rate of efficiency of the rater given in the problem.

(i) Time taken for Activity 'A'

$6 \times (200/1300) \times (120/10) = 1.1$

(ii) Time Taken for Activity 'B'

$6 \times (300/1300) \times (90/100) = 1.2$

(iii) Time Taken for Activity 'C'

$6 \times (500/1300) \times (80/100) = 1.8$

(iv) Time Taken for Activity 'D'

$6 \times (100/1300) \times (70/100) = 0.3$

Total Normal Time = 4.4

Now, we have to compute Standard Time using this formula:

(Total Activity-wise Time or Normal Time/ {1- Personal Fraction Time})

i.e. $4.4/(1 - 0.1) = 4.4/0.9 = 4.8$ minutes.

10.5.2B *Dearness Allowance (DA)*

To give effect to price neutralisation, DA is paid over and above the basic wages to ensure that real income of the workers is not falling short. There are several methods of computation of DA, which can be enumerated as follows:

1. DA not linked to Consumer Price Index:

    a. Flat DA

    b. Graduated Scale of D.A.

2. Linked to Consumer Price Index:

    a. DA computed according to changes in C.P.I.

    b. DA linked to pay scales and to C.P.I

Supreme Court of India has laid down certain criteria for regulating payment of DA as under:

1. Capacity to Pay

2. Rates prevailing in comparable concerned in the region

3. Extent of neutralisation of price rise

The views of the National Labour Commission are:

1. The basic wages in all cases should be adjusted to a common base year.

2. DA should be adjusted every time when there is a 5 point change in the C.P.I.

3. Neutralisation should be allowed at the rate of 95 per cent in the non-scheduled employment.

4. Capacity to pay is irrelevant for payment of DA at the minimum level.

10.6 OVERTIME WAGES

Overtime wages are calculated on the basis of the working hours prescribed to the several types of workmen. If 36 hours a week are prescribed as working hours, the company should pay extra wages to workmen if they are required to work beyond 36 hours. Usually the rate of wages for period beyond 36 hours should be at the ordinary rate, while the rate should be double if the workers are required to work more than 48 hours a week for the period beyond 48 hours. However, where wages are paid on a piece-rate basis, the State Government in consultation with the employer concerned and the representatives of the workers, shall fix the time-rate as nearly as possible, considering average rate of earnings of those workers and the rates so fixed shall be deemed to be the ordinary rate of wages of the workers and hence, overtime rate should be decided following the above principles.

10.7 INCENTIVE SCHEMES

Incentives are paid to the workmen over and above the normal wages to reward their good performance. In places, where piece-rate system of wages are existing, payment of incentives is relatively simple as for manufacturing additional units than the standard one, workers can be paid extra wages, which they are supposed to get for each additional unit. This incentive scheme is known as Straight Piece-Rate Scheme. In time-rate system, however, such incentives are computed following Standard Hour Systems. To illustrate, let us assume a given volume of job is given to a worker for standard 8 hours' work. If the worker is able to complete the job with in 6 hours, then for hours saved, i.e. 2 hours, he should be given the incentives duly upgrading his hourly wage rate apportioning his 8 hours rate for 6 hours. Let us assume 8 hours are needed as standard time for completing a job and the rate per hour is Rs 1/-. If the worker finishes the work in 6 hours, he will also get Rs 8/-, which upgrades his hourly wage rate then from Rs 1/- to Rs 1.33.

There are several other Incentive Schemes too, which can be briefly stated as follows:

(i) **Barth System:** Under this system, there is no minimum guaranteed wage. The formula (considering hourly wage rate of Rs 1/-) is as follows:

Wage = Std time 8hrs x time taken (6 hrs) x hourly rate Rs 1/- = Rs 7/- (approx.)

(ii) **Bedaux System**: This system is also called 'units' or 'points' system. It has a guaranteed basic rate like the Halsey and Rowan Systems. Under this system each minute or Standard Time is expressed in terms of units or points after a detailed time study. The guaranteed basic wage is paid upto 60 points per hour scored by the worker. Points earned above 60 are paid at 75 to 100 per cent of the basic wage rate (the standard daily rate for the job which is always higher than the minimum guaranteed wage).

(iii) **Taylorian System**: In this scheme there are two piece-rates one lower and one higher plus a bonus paid as a percentage of the time rate. Obviously such a system would automatically discourage low production and would be installed where the average performance is well below expectations.

(iv) **Merrick Differential Piece Rate System:** Under this system there are three piece rates-

a. Upto, say, 83 per cent of standard output - piece-rate + 10 per cent of time rate as bonus.

b. Above 83 per cent and upto 100 per cent of standard output - same piece rate + 20 per cent of time rate.

c. Above 100 per cent of standard output -same piece rate but no bonus.

(v) *Gantt Task System:* This has three stages of payment:

a. Below the standard performance, only the minimum guaranteed wage is to be paid.

b. At the standard performance, this wage + 20 per cent of the time rate will be paid as bouns.

c. When the standard is exceeded, higher piece-rate is paid but there is no bonus.

The main objective of this scheme is to raise the performance upto the standard level which is the task set before the workers.

(vi) *The Emerson Empiric System:* Under this system, standard time is established for each job. The efficiency of the worker is determined by dividing the time taken into the standard time. Upto 67 per cent efficiency the worker is paid at this time rate and from this point to 100 per cent a bonus of 1 per cent is paid for every additional 1 per cent output. At 100 per cent efficiency, a bonus of 20 per cent is paid.

(vii) *Accelerating Premium System:* This provides for a guaranteed minimum wage for output below the standard. For low and average increase in output above the standard small increments in earnings are allowed. Increasingly large earnings are conceded for the above average output, the increment being different for each 1 per cent increase in output.

(viii) *Scablon Plan*: The Scablon Plan was designed to involve the workers in making suggestions for reducing the cost of operation and improving the working methods and sharing in the gains of increased productivity. The Rucker Plan is similar to the Scablon Plan, the only difference being that in the latter the incentive earnings are calculated on the basis of the 'value added' by the manufacturing process. The Kaiser Plan is also like these – a gains-sharing scheme. While the Rucker Plan excludes all the supply and material costs, the Kaiser Plan excludes all costs over which the workers have no control.

(ix) *Halsey Premium Plan*: It guarantees a fixed time wage to slow workers and, at the same time, offers extra pay to efficient workers. Extra pay in the form of bonus is given based on the amount of time saved by the worker, which is calculated @ 33-1/2 per cent of the time saved. Thus, the cost of labour is reduced because of the percentage premium system.

(x) *Rowan Premium Plan*: Under this plan, the time saved is expressed as a percentage of the time allowed and the hourly rate of pay is increased by that percentage so that total earnings of the worker are the total number of hours multiplied by the increased hourly wages.

10.8 FRINGE BENEFITS

The fringe benefits have often been described as 'welfare expenses', 'wage supplements', 'perquisites other than wages', 'sub-wages' and 'social charges'. ILO has defined fringe benefits as under: "Wages are often augmented by special cash benefits, by the provision of medical and other services or by payments in kind that form part of the wage for expenditure or other goods and services". In addition, workers commonly receive such benefits as holidays with pay, low-cost meals, low rent housing, etc. Such additions to the wage proper are sometimes referred to as 'fringe benefits'. However, it is important to note that 'benefits' which have no relation to employment or wages should not be regarded as 'fringe benefits', despite the fact it may constitute a significant part of workers total income. Fringe benefits account for the services rendered to workers and their families by an industrial enterprise for the purpose of raising their moral, material, social and cultural levels and to prepare them for a better life.

Thus, fringe benefits can broadly be classified under six main heads as under:

(i)   Extra payment for time worked (overtime, weekend holidays, shift premiums, etc.).

(ii)   Payment for time not worked (lunch period and rest time, medical care time, sick leave, maternity leave, death in family leave, grievance handling, voting time, paid holidays and vacations, severance pay and lay-off, etc).

(iii)   Monetary prizes for special activities and performance anniversary award, quality bonus, waste reduction, safety awards, attendance bonus, suggestion plan award, etc.

(iv)   Bonus Payments

(v)   Payment for personal security and financial protection - medical care, old-age pension, unemployment insurance, family allowance, compensation for disability and death, housing, room and board allowance, etc.

(vi)   Payment for the welfare facilities like maintaining dining room, cultural and recreational facilities, etc.

10.9 EMPLOYEE SERVICES

These services are those which are provided by the organisations, in addition to the usual fringe benefits, either at no cost to the employee or at highly subsidised rate. Such services include eating facilities, transportation facilities, child care facilities, educational services, flexible working hours, etc.

REVIEW QUESTIONS

1.   What are the important objectives of a Wage Policy? Distinguish between Fair Wages and Living Wages.

2.   Describe some important techniques of Wage Determination.

3.   To what extent Job Evaluation technique is useful for Wage Determination? What are the different types of Job Evaluation? Which type you consider better and why?

4.   Describe the role of Time Study in Wage Determination.

5.   Describe various incentive schemes. Which are the incentive schemes you consider better for employee motivation.

6.   What way fringe benefits help in employee motivation?

11 EMPLOYEE DISCIPLINE AND GRIEVANCE HANDLING

LEARNING OBJECTIVES

This chapter will help in developing:

☐ different approaches to the problem of discipline

☐ steps to ensure discipline in organisations

☐ methodology to handle discipline with a positive approach

☐ role of personnel administration to enforce discipline

☐ greivance handling procedures

CONTENT OUTLINE

11.1 INTRODUCTION

In broad sense, discipline means orderly and systematic behaviour. Every organisation, for operative efficiency, frames certain codes of behaviour for employees, under normal practice, contract or statutes or under mutual understanding. Breaking of such behavioural norms creates disciplinary problems.

Zack and Bloch devised the theory of Progressive Discipline, leaving the burden of improvement entirely on the workers. Such philosophy helps the management to perceive discipline as a mechanical process. On the other hand, Corrective Discipline demands the sharing of responsibility by both employees and the supervisors. While to comply with work standards is the responsibility of workers, the responsibility of supervisors is to create the environment of like nature. Following steps are important for Corrective Discipline:

    a. Early intervention
    b. Identification of problem
    c. Clear expectations
    d. Feedback
    e. Positive reinforcement
    f. Follow-up

Corrective discipline is ideally suited to solve continual performance problems, rather than isolated ones. Discipline again may be classified as Positive discipline and Negative discipline. When a person spontaneously abides by the required norms, it is called Positive or Constructive discipline. But when he is compelled to behave in a desired way under threat or fear of punishment, it is termed as Negative, Punitive or Autocratic discipline.

Positive discipline is achieved through education and training and Negative discipline is enforced by punishment. Indiscipline may be of two types: Individual or Collective. Individual causes are basically a problem of attitude, while industrial relations are responsible for Corrective indiscipline.

11.2 THEORIES OF DISCIPLINARY POWERS

Employers derive their disciplinary power presumably from two theories: Institutional Theory and Contractual Theory.

(i) *Institutional Theory:* Organisation structure is designed in a hierarchical manner. Employers being the head assume highest responsibility to look after the interests of such organised community. As such, they feel that they have the power to make regulations, direct operations and exercise disciplinary control.

(ii) *Contractual Theory:* This theory, however, considers that employers' disciplinary powers stem from the contract of employment. Employment contracts subject employees to subordination and thereby vest employers with necessary authority to ensure performance, which again is possible by enforcement of disciplinary powers.

11.3 DIFFERENT APPROACHES TO THE PROBLEM OF DISCIPLINE

Indiscipline and violence can be diagnosed from the following approaches:

(i) Legalistic approach

(ii) Humanitarian approach

(iii) Human Resource approach

(iv) Behavioural approach

(v) Leadership approach

Legalistic approach being too formal and rigid can hardly bring about changes in workers' mind. The concept is somewhat like progressive discipline. Other approaches are important as by taking care, we can minimise the recurrence of such ill-fated behaviour, subject to its proper enforcement. The other four approaches are interlinked, hence, we are not disaggregating the approaches, rather trying to analyse from an aggregative angle.

Causes of indiciplined behaviour are usually:

a. Excessive job pressure,

b. Improper training,

c. Ignored complaints,

d. Unfair treatment,

e. Favouritism,

f. Poor management-labour relations,

g. Lack of confident leadership,

h. Lack of recognition and lack of opportunity for initiative.

V.K. Calla, in his *Discipline In Industry*, has identified seven reasons for disobeying as follows:

a. Ignorance,

b. Physical or mental incapacity,

c. Inadequate training,

d. Dissatisfaction in work,

e. Misguidance of Union,

f. Desperate attempt to claim self leadership by deliberate dissonance and

g. Absence of standard or uniform disciplinary policy.

To identify indiscipline in the organisation, Calla further mentioned some indicators, like:

a. High rate of absenteeism

b. High rate of labour turnover

c. High rate of sickness and accidents

d. Multiple unresolved grievances

e. Industrial Relations state.

f. Low output, faulty out-turn and lower productivity

g. Low motivation and morale

h. Prevalence of 'we-feeling' in the work-group, etc.

We-feeling in a strict sense means dominance of individual identity over organisational identity.

11.3.1 Disciplinary Probelms

Poor handling of disciplinary action may cause serious problems to the organisation. Although nature of the problem varies from organisation to organisation (due to difference in size, structure, management style and ownership), common problems may be summed up as follows:

(i) Increase in the number of cases to arbitration (including cases hard to defend), thereby raising cost both in terms of arbitration fees and work stoppages (due to loss of working hours of both the aggrieved employees and their witnesses).

(ii) Increase in the cost of training and recruitment for high labour turnover. Failure of the organisation to set right grievances with proper intervention frustrates the employees and at times they withdraw from the organisation either on their own or on organisational order. This leads to colossal loss, particularly in terms of training cost, which the organisation sustains either in a formal way (through training in outside institutions) or in an informal way (learning while at work).

(iii) Increase in frequent work disruptions cause production loss, create an adverse impact on market for non-compliance of purchasers' delivery schedules and thereby affects profitability.

(iv) Increase in hostility and loss of self-respect vitiate organisational culture, develop mistrust, which in turn seriously impedes productivity.

This necessitates proper handling of employee complaints, a checklist of which may be devised as follows:

a. Put the aggrieved employee at ease.

b. Communicate your gladness for his coming.

c. Ask what he or she would like to discuss.

d. Listen attentively.

e. Sympathise with the employee.

f. Explain what you expect to do.

g. Set a follow up date.

11.3.2 Norms to ensure Discipline in organisations

By now it is clear that to ensure discipline in an organisation, set of norms needs to be followed. Such basic pre-requisites are as follows:

(i) The goals or objectives should be stated clearly. The rules must be in clear and unambiguous terms, with special mention of the standards expected of the workmen.

(ii) Such rules and regulations should be properly communicated and must be understood.

(iii) The authority to enforce rules must be specified.

(iv) The procedure for appeal by an aggrieved party should be specified.

(v) Punishment prescribed should be made known.

(vi) The rules of conduct must contain provisions for investigation and settlement of grievances.

11.3.3 Causal factors of indiscipline

Problem of indiscipline is the culmination of multiple factors; for precisive solutions we need to consider the exact causal factor instrumental for indisciplinary behaviour of employees. In fact the causal factors may be:

(1) the employee himself,

(2) the supervisor or,

(3) the organisation.

Employees indisciplined behaviour largely stems from the organisation itself. However, such employees too are not uncommon who, because of their intrinsic characteristics (which build their habit, strength and personality) by nature are aggrieved easily and nurture indiscipline, whose percentage though minute may influence the attitudes of other members of the organisation (at conscious or unconscious level) and thereby threaten smooth functioning of the organisation.

The supervisor may be the causal factor for inappropriate method of supervision and giving improper assignments and orders. The organisation becomes a causal factor with the use of unsound and unnecessarily restrictive policies and regulations and with improper expectations from the employees.

The organisation, to mitigate this problem, should:

(i) apply its rules with fair objectivity or uniformly,

(ii) communicate to employees the consequences of their actions and

(iii) adopt fair rules and directives and expect from employees reasonably.

Similarly supervisors, to minimise the problem of indisciplines should

(i) avoid inappropriate action in matching offences with sanctions,

(ii) ensure due to process and equal protection as means of creating an organisational culture that supports employees' dignity and rights,

(iii) minimise the need for employees to pursue their rights through external channels such as Arbitration, Government and Courts.

11.3.4 Need for a Disciplinary Policy

To obviate the problem of indiscipline, every organisation should have a well defined disciplinary policy. A well defined "....... Discipline Policy avoids management inconsistencies and promotes a climate of mutual respect, fair play and clear standards throughout the organisation." Disciplinary Policy to a great extent stands on prevailing norms and legal requirements. But to make it more effective, management can instill its own philosophy (with more humanitarian approach). Such a step will make the policy more flexible than a rigid or formal one, which perceives man as a passive organism. While framing a disciplinary policy, following principles should be followed:

1. A searching examination for the cause of indiscipline should always be made.

2. Disciplinary rules should be framed after due consultation with the workers or their representatives.

3. If any particular rule is infringed frequently, its causes should be investigated.

4. Rules should be considered as means and not as ends. Thus, rules should not be rigid.

5. Periodically rules should be checked-up to understand whether changes are necessary in the light of the experience.

6. Rules should be enforced without any bias.

7. Rules should be strictly complied by the management people to set an example before others to emulate.

11.4 ROLE OF TRADE UNIONS IN DISCIPLINE

Trade Unions to a great extent are responsible for indiscipline and violence, particularly in organisations which are unionised and where multiple unions exist. Different philosophies of trade unionism or different schools of thought perceive management differently. Their expectations too at times vary. Thus, the Economic Advantage School believes in maximisation of wage gains. The Job Security School believes that long term security of employment is more important than short run maximisation of wages. The Marxist School perceives conflict between capital and labour is inherent. The Political School emphasises power conflict between management and labour over different basic issues such as the recognition of unions, collective bargaining procedures, jurisdictional disputes, etc. The Human Relations School is concerned with power and status. Such divergent schools of thought widely differ in their approaches. Unless management tries to integrate their own philosophies with trade unions, industrial relations are likely to deteriorate which subsequently give rise to indisciplined and violent behaviour.

However, the influence of affiliated trade unions in industrial disputes in India does not seem to be a major problem, when we try to corroborate with statistical data. Unaffiliated unions and others percentage share to total disputes in India, on an average is 85.23 per cent, percentage share of workers involved is 84.37 per cent and finally percentage share to total man-days loss is 93.7 percent.

11.5 STEPS TO ENFORCE DISCIPLINARY PROCEDURE

A systematic disciplinary procedure is essential to maintain established standards of work. Following steps are followed to enforce discipline in an organisation:

1. Calling for explanation

2. Consideration of explanation

3. Show-cause notice

4. Notice of holding the enquiry

5. The holding of enquiry

6. Punishment

7. Follow-up

11.6 DISCIPLINE WITHOUT PUNISHMENT

John Huberman in his famous article *Discipline without Punishment* spelt out the methodologies to handle disciplinary problems in organisation with a positive disciplinary approach. He has suggested the following course of action to rectify the indisciplined behaviour of employees in organisations:

1. No disciplinary demotions, suspensions or other forms of punishment be applied.

2. In case of disciplinary problems which may consequently give rise to unsatisfactory work performance (e.g. carelessness in handling materials, less attention to duty) or break of discipline (e.g. overstaying rest or lunch periods, absenting from duty, etc.) following steps should be followed:

   a. The immediate superior will offer the worker a casual and friendly reminder on the job.

   b. If the incident continues to recur, the boss will again try to correct it calling the individual to his office for a serious but friendly chat. The boss at this stage will explain the need for and purpose of the rules, make sure the employee understands the same.

   c. In case of further repetition of the incidents, earlier step should further be repeated with some variation like verifying from the employee whether he is disliking the work. If that be the case, the employee may be told that it is better for him to look for some other job or line of work. This conversation may be further confirmed in a letter to employee's home.

   d. If the employee continues to be indisciplined even after 6 to 8 weeks from this period, he should be asked to go home with pay to consider seriously whether he does or does not wish to abide by the company standards. At this time he should be informed that recurrence of such behaviour will result to his termination.

   e. If another incident occurs even after this, the employee's services are terminated.

Huberman contended this approach to a significant extent changes the indisciplined behaviour of the employee and thus without directly taking any punitive measures, rectification/correction of the employees indisciplined behaviour becomes possible.

Opposed to this approach, we have McGregor's Hot Stove Rule, which suggested infringing discipline should invite direct punitive measures to rectify the behaviour. Since we do not have sufficient study to authenticate which disciplinary action is more appropriate, it is difficult to suggest a particular approach to handle disciplinary problems in Indian organisations.

11.7 RESULTS OF SURVEY ON DISCIPLINARY PROBLEMS

The author in his individual capacity has carried out a survey on Disciplinary Policy, as it is still now a dreaded causal factor of industrial disputes in India claiming maximum number of loss of man-days. The survey was carried out during 1995 covering 25 Personnel Managers, 50 Supervisors and 100 Workers of different trades drawn from 17 organisations, including public sector organisations. For the purpose of the survey separate set of structured questionnaires were made covering following areas:

1. Relations with fellow workers
2. Cooperation that they receive from co-workers
3. Perception about working conditions
4. Feelings about pay packets
5. Job satisfaction
6. Independent responsibility in job
7. Extent of agreement with management's ideas
8. Whether suggestions honoured by Management
9. Feelings about the style of supervision
10. Knowledge and attitude towards company's disciplinary policies
11. Uniformity of policies - whether some get special privilege
12. Grievance handling procedures
13. Time usually taken for grievance redressal
14. Attitudes towards union
15. Perception of gherao and use of abusive language
16. Distribution of domestic hours and holidays

Survey results have been grouped into two aspects : Positive and Negative. A note on Public Sectors has been given separately for obvious differences in work culture and organisational pattern with Private Sectors. Management-union-worker relationship has also been shown separately and finally a conclusion has been drawn in the light of the survey to ensure discipline in an organisation.

11.7.1 Positive Aspects of Survey

1. A sense of belonging develops even in organisations where workers are not well paid because of their association with company over a long period. Such feelings debar workers from being violent or agitated.

2. If the company can fruitfully convince workers about the present situation, which prevents management from acceding to workers' demand for higher wages, workers are prepared to sacrifice their present for future betterment.

3. A positive behavioural reinforcement helps management to accept workers' demand with some deviations without any effect on workers' discipline.

4. Institutional culture and prevalence of family hierarchical relations have positive effect on workers' discipline.

5. Friendly relations with open door policy dissuade workers from being indisciplined.

6. An intrinsically indisciplined worker cannot remain in the group for long. The group in such cases often creates pressure on management to isolate such an element.

7. Communications in workers' language have positive effects on workers' behaviour.

8. Quick disposal of grievances is possible by forming joint worker-management committees at every operational level. Settlement of disputes at the originating level does not allow indiscipline to spread.

9. Absence of hierarchical barrier has positive effect on workers' discipline.

10. Slackened disciplinary policy, if followed uniformly, boosts worker's loyalty towards organisation and keeps them in abeyance from being indisciplined on future issues.

11.7.2 Negative Aspects

1. Improper job distribution (where some are allowed to remain idle or given minimum job while some others are burdened with job pressure) aggrieves workers in general.

2. Frequent changes of executives confuse workers as they are subjected to divergent approaches. This situation negatively affects workers' behaviour.

3. Workers view seriously when they are not allowed to approach higher officials for redressal of their grievance but receive orders directly from the top to execute jobs. This induces them to be indisciplined by disobeying orders or to justify their importance.

4. Simultaneous orders from different levels confuse workers and adversely affect discipline.

5. Young educated workers are more indisciplined than old illiterate ones.

6. A sense of insecurity regarding future existence of the organisation impairs productivity and depress workers. Such depression, if it is acute, takes the shape of violence.

7. Incomplete communication about company's rules and regulations confuses workers and supervisors exercising their discretion in matters of leave sanction, overtime or acceptance of late comers. Disfavoured employees for obvious reason get dissatisfied and consequently nurture indiscipline.

8. Workers do not tolerate management's high-handed attitude indefinitely. They react on continuance.

9. Casual and *badli* workers are more indisciplined and violent in nature.

10. Workers in general become indisciplined due to prevalence of excessive noise, bad sanitation and improper humidification (causing much discomfort for intolerable heat) in workplaces.

11. Workers, satisfied financially, look for other comforts in workplaces and such issues, if not considered by management, cause dissatisfaction. Such dissatisfaction develops indisciplined attitude.

11.8 SOME POINTS ABOUT PUBLIC SECTOR

1. Workers in public sector, for the obvious sense of service security, face the management even with minor discords. They, however, feel management can do nothing beyond defining rules and regulations.

2. Management is more biased in the public sector. 'Robbing Peter to pay Paul' recurs often, causing great harm to industrial relations.

3. Public Sector seriously lacks in management expertise or professionalism to handle employee grievances. Even problems soluble within the organisation are left unattended, allowing aggravation of situation and virtually employees are forced to take resort to the long-drawn legal system.

11.9 STEPS TO ENSURE DISCIPLINE

1. Delegate authority for grievance handling (minor in nature) at operation level, forming group or committee with workers, unions and management's representatives.

2. Allow dissatisfied employees to represent their case in person to higher authorities (with suitable control).

3. Introduce suitable training packages as a continuous process for in-job development. Such training should adequately be value laden.

4. Follow a standing disciplinary policy strictly framed after discussion with workers and adequately complying with legal requirements. Such policy should be communicated to each and every worker.

5. Supervisors should know the extent of their authority. Any exercise of discretion causing dissatisfaction among others should be strictly debarred.

6. Organisational environment, responsible for workers' disgruntlement should be immediately looked into. Changes in line with requirements should be undertaken. If it is impossible for any technical reason or paucity of funds, communication to that effect should be made to the workers.

7. Orders for job execution should flow to workers from one channel only.

8. Job distribution should be proper.

11.9.1 Role of Personnel Administrator to enforce Discipline

1. To advise and assist top and line management to adopt and develop constructive management philosophy regarding employees and their conduct.

2. To assist in formulation of effective and positive disciplinary policy and procedure.

3. To communicate the policies to all the employees in the organisation.

4. To ensure that disciplinary policies and procedures are conforming to the legal provisions.

5. To enforce the policies strictly in an unbiased manner.

6. To ensure that disciplinary action is consistent with the principles of Personnel Management.

7. To train executives and supervisors in handling disciplinary problems and cases.

8. To involve the union and employees in the formulation and implementation of disciplinary process and measures.

9. To help to develop standards of self discipline among the employees.

10. To win the confidence of employees in company policies and discipline.

11.9.2 Disciplinary Proceedings (Domestic Enquiry) Steps

11.9.2A *Complaint*

A written complaint from the Supervisor about the commission of the act of misconduct is the starting point. This should give details of time, place and the incident.

11.9.2B *Framing of Charge-sheet*

a. The charge-sheet should be drafted in a clear and unambiguous language.

b. If the charge relates to an incident, date, time and place of occurrence should be mentioned.

c. The charge-sheet calling upon the employee to submit an explanation must specify the period of time by which the employee has to submit his explanation.

11.9.2C *Suspension Pending Enquiry*

If the act of misconduct is very serious, the employee may be suspended pending enquiry. It has to be made clear that during the period of suspension, pending enquiry, he will not leave station. Subsistence allowance is payable to him under the rules. He should give a declaration that he is not employed else where during that period.

11.9.2D *Issue of Charge-sheet*

The charge-sheet should be served personally with acknowledgement. If he refuses to accept, the same should be sent to his local and home address under registered post A.D. as well as under certificate of posting. If the charge-sheet is returned undelivered, the envelope should be kept without opening. In this situation a copy of the charge-sheet should be displayed on the notice board.

11.9.2E *Consideration of Explanation*

a. The charge-sheeted employee may admit the charge and request for mercy; or

b. He may deny the charge and request for enuiry; or

c. He may not reply at all.

11.9.2F *Enquiry Proceedings*

a. If the charge is minor and the workman begs to be excused, no enquiry is required.

b. If his misconduct is serious enough to warrant discharge or dismissal, a proper enquiry is to be held before awarding punishment.

c. If he fails to submit the reply within specified time limit, steps should be taken to hold the enquiry. While issuing the notice for the enquiry, the employee should be requested to submit his explanation.

d. The enquiry officer should give full opportunity to the employee to defend himself by cross-examining the witnesses produced by the management.

e. It is for the management to prove the charges against a workman and it is not the workman who has to prove his innocence.

11.9.2G *Co-worker's Assistance*

Depending on the provisions of Standing Orders and Service rules a co-worker may be allowed to help the employee in domestic enquiry.

11.9.2H *Exparte Enquiry*

If the employee fails to turn up for the enquiry after being given sufficient notice, the enquiry officer may conduct the enquiry and take evidence as required.

11.9.2I *Enquiry Report*

The enquiry officer, after having gone through the entire records of the proceedings and giving his reasons for accepting or rejecting any evidence tendered in the course of enquiry, has to categorically state whether the charges are proved or not proved. He has to submit a written report giving his verdict and recommendation together with the reasons.

11.9.2J *Final Action*

The Competent Authority will go through the enquiry report and all connected papers/ exhibits and has the option to agree or disagree with the findings of the enquiry officer. If he does not agree, he has to give reasons before drawing his conclusions and awarding punishment. The employee should be informed in writing of the punishment.

11.10 GRIEVANCE HANDLING

Grievance is defined as 'cause for complaints or annoyance'. Initially Grievance Handling was a one-step procedure. The worker directly approached the employer and a decision was given immediately. However, with the development of mass production facilities, increased number of workers and supervisors and complication of multi-tier organisational structure, number of grievances in organisations have gone up considerably making it difficult to sustain grievance handling as a one-step procedure.

The best way to handle grievance is to deal with it in the shortest possible time and at the lowest possible level. Unfortunately not many establishments have a formal, laid-out procedure for dealing with grievances. In grievance handling, the role of Personnel Manager should be purely advisory and every effort should be made to induct and train each supervisor in handling the grievances of his subordinates effectively.

11.10.1 Grievance handling Procedure

The step-ladder procedure of Grievance Handling is a widely used technique. The stages are as follows:

1. The aggrieved employee approaches the immediate supervisor either in person or through a written application in a standard form within a week's time, i.e. from the period when he feels certain action of the management has resulted in a sense of grievance in him. The immediate supervisor (in accordance with the delegated authority and the type of grievance) discuss the grievance with the employee and gives his decision. A time limit of two weeks can be given for this stage.

2. If the employee is not satisfied with the decision in the first stage, he may approach the departmental head with a written application in a standard form, for reconsideration of his case. The employee may be allowed to personally

represent the case along with the co-worker. The departmental head should give his decision in 15 days' time.

3. The appeals at this stage would be handled by a Joint Committee consisting of an equal number of representatives of the union and management. A secretariat is provided to process the cases at this stage. This committee should also have a time-limit for appeals as well as for disposal of the grievance referred to it. This committee shall give its recommendation by consensus and agreement. Unanimous recommendations of the committee shall be accepted by the management who must issue orders accordingly. The union and management may also reverse the right not to accept the recommendations and should convey their views within three days of receipt of the recommendations. Otherwise it should be deemed to have been accepted by both. In the event of non-acceptance of the recommendations by either party or non-unanimity in the committee at this stage, the grievance may be forwarded by the committee to a high-level Joint Committee.

4. At this stage the joint committee shall consist of top management and union representatives. Cases spilling over from the above stage as well as those brought up by either side will be considered and decisions taken for implementation. If disagreements still prevail, both the sides may refer it for arbitration.

With sincerity of purpose and an intention to resolve disagreements across the table a formalised procedure as above is bound to result in achievement of industrial harmony.

The above model Grievance Handling Procedure was adopted in the 16th Session of the Indian Labour Conference in 1958 as part of the Code of Discipline in a volunatry measure. Many progressive organisations have adopted the system with suitable modifications.

11.10.2 Principles of Natural Justice

In a series of decisions, the Supreme Court made certain observations in dealing with delinquent employees. These are known as Rules of Natural Justice and require that:

1. The employee proceeded against must be informed clearly of the charges levelled against him.

2. The witnesses must be examined ordinarily in the presence of the charge-sheeted employee, in respect of the charges.

3. The employee must be given fair opportunity to cross-examine the witneses.

4. The enquiry officer has to record his findings along with the reasons for the same in his report.

REVIEW QUESTIONS

1. What are the steps necessary for Corrective Discipline? How Positive Discipline approach is different from Negative Discipline? Which approach you consider best?

2. What are the causes of indisciplined behaviour in an organisation?

3. Briefly state common disciplinary problems. Prepare a checklist for resolving such problems.

4. Develop a Disciplinary Policy for an organisation covering at least four important areas.

5. What are the steps one should follow in initiating disciplinary action against an employee?

6. Discuss step-ladder system in Grievance Handling.

12 COLLECTIVE BARGAINING

LEARNING OBJECTIVES

This chapter discusses:

- ☐ essential features and importance of collective bargaining
- ☐ pre-requisites of collective bargaining
- ☐ collective bargaining in India

CONTENT OUTLINE

12.1 INTRODUCTION

ILO defines the term Collective Bargaining as 'negotiations about working conditions and terms of employment between an employer, a group of employers or one or more employers' organisations, on the one hand and/or more representatives of workers organisation on the other hand with a view to reach an agreement'.

In collective bargaining, the object is to arrive at an agreement on wages and other conditions of employment about which the parties start with divergent view points, but ultimately attempt to make a compromise. As soon as the bargain is made, the terms of agreement are put into operation. On the other hand, the major task of the latter relates to sharing the information and suggestions with regard to issues of common interests including health, safety, welfare and productive efficiency.

Mary Sur observes, collective bargaining starts with claims advanced by both sides demands from the union and statements by the management on how far they can concede these demands and what they want in return, just as the bazaar vendor and buyer start by quoting prices which are at variance, each knowing that he will have to make some accommodation in the end in order to reach a final agreed price. According to Encyclopaedia of Social Sciences - 'Collective Bargaining is a process of discussion and negotiation between two parties, one or both of whom is a group of persons acting in concert. The resulting bargain is an understanding as to the terms and conditions under which a continuing service is to be performed .... More specifially, collective bargaining is a procedure by which employers and a group of employees agree upon the conditions of work'.

12.2 CHARACTERISTICS OF COLLECTIVE BARGAINING

From the foregoing definitions of collective bargaining, some essential characteristics may be enumerated as follows:

a. It is a group action as opposed to individual action and initiated through the representatives of workers and delegates of the management at the bargaining table.

b. It is flexible and mobile and not fixed or static. It has flexibility and ample scope for compromise for a mutual give and take before the final agreement.

c. It is a two party process. It can succeed only when both labour and management want to succeed. There must be a mutual eagerness to develop the collective bargaining procedure and result in a harmony and progress. It can flourish only in an atmosphere which is free from animosity and reprisal.

d. It is a continuous process, which provides a mechanism for continuing and organised relationships between management and trade unions. The heart of collective bargaining is the process for continuing joint consideration and adjustment of plant and problems.

e. The term is dynamic itself because the concept is growing, expanding and changing.

f. It is industrial democracy at work.

g. It is not a competitive process by a complementary process, i.e. each party needs something that the other party has, viz, labour can made a greater productive effort and management has the capacity to pay.

h. It is an art, an advanced form of human relations. To substantiate this one need only witness the bluffing, the oratory, dramatics and coyness mixed in an inexplicable fashion which may characterise a bargaining session.

12.2.1 Importance and need for Collective Bargaining

It is evident from the foregoing discussion that to settle differences on the work related issues, Collective Bargaining as a process is perceived both by employers and employees as an important machinery. We have adequately covered the general issues which are usually settled through collective bargaining.

The need for collective bargaining in India arose due to some controversial problems which the Indian industry had to face after the termination of the second world war. One of the most important among these is that of modernisation. The problems of modernisation and productivity are to be viewed in a proper light in the context of industrial development on planned lines. Indian industry cannot compete in foreign markets if it does not follow modern methods of production. Since modernisation causes displacement of workers, it naturally invites hostility and the workers and management must, therefore, come together in their viewpoint through collective bargaining. The solution of common problems can come from legislative measures. Collective agreements provide the climate for smooth progress as there is ample scope for a synthesis between demands from one side and concessions from the other.

(i)   In individual bargaining the workers may be tempted to accept undesirable conditions and may thus bring down in general level of remuneration. Due to immobility of labour all workers are not in a position to desert a wage cutting employer. This immobility may be due to ignorance and illiteracy and industry specific skill factors.

(ii) The speedy workers may accept a lower rate of payment which may yield them a reasonable amount of wages, but such a low rate of wages would yield insufficient earnings to a great majority of workers.

(iii) Sometimes employers are in a position to control the bulk demands for the labourers and they may through combined action, force the workers to accept low wages. Collective bargaining is the only device which can avert such combined action and prevent the creation of such monopolistic tendencies.

(iv) The market apparatus consisting of the two forces of demand and supply can settle only the problem of determination of wages, some of the non-wages issues like the length of working day, health and safety of workers, speed operations, introduction of rationalisation measures of security of job have to be settled by personal decisions and not by the forces of demand and supply.

(v) Collective bargaining also provides some voice in the conduct and management of the industry. Workers have now a definite place in the exercise of a real influence in the determination of labour matters affecting them every now and then.

(vi) To ensure continuity of production, workers and employers must shake hands and this makes it inevitable to make collective bargaining a regular feature of industrial life.

(vii) The problem of good human relations can be tackled successfully by Collective Bargaining Process.

12.2.2 Pre-requisites for Collective Bargaining

The success of collective bargaining machinery largely depends on the respective attitudes of workers in general and union in particular on one hand and the attitude of management or employer on the other. However, if collective bargaining is to exist in the country successfully the following factors are essential:

1. It is necessary for the management to recognise the union and to bargain in more good faith, in the unionised situations. This is also pressure on the union to formulate plans and demands in a systematic manner.

2. There should be a change in the attitude of employers and employees. They must realise that collective bargaining approach does not imply litigation as it does under adjudication. It should be kept in mind of both that, they are to resolve their differences on their respective claims quitely and calmly, with their own resources, reducing their dependence on the third party intervention.

3. For the purpose of collective bargaining, employers should be represented by the management and workers by their union representatives. Careful thought and selection of the negotiating team is very much essential. For management team, it is better to have a mixed composition, such as production, finance, industrial relation experts and headed by a personnel expert.

4. It is also appreciable to have open minds, listening others' concern and point of view and to have some flexibility in making adjustments to the demands.

5. To ensure collective bargaining, unfair labour practices should be avoided and abandoned by both otherwise atmosphere and confidence will be vitiated by malpractices if either side takes advantage of the other by resorting to unfair practices.

6. Either side should avoid to put any irrational or unreasonable demand.

7. Negotiations can be successful only when the parties rely on facts and figures to support their point of view. That is why trade union should be assisted by specialists, viz., economists, productivity experts, etc.

8. Trade union should encourage the internal union democracy and periodic consultation with the general file of the union members.

9. The negotiations results, the terms of contract should be in writing and embodied in a document. If no agreement is reached the parties should proceed to conciliation, mediation or arbitration.

If no settlement is arrived at even then, the workers should be free to go in for strike and the employers on lockout. But utmost care should be taken to resolve differences mutually.

10. Strike and lockouts should be the last resort. Periodic discussions may be necessary between management and unions to interpret the provisions of the contract and clarify doubts.

11. Trade Unions should be equally concerned with both quality of work, both leading upto a consistent concern for the viability of the firm and its products and services.

12. Once the agreement is reached, it must be honoured and fairly implemented.

12.2.3 Collective Bargaining in India

There are certain differences in union characteristics in developed and developing countries. In UK, workers are unionised as per their respective trades. Such unionisation which is other way more concerned for the group well being in reality provided the base for bargaining with management on different employment issues.

The term collective bargaining in fact originated from Great Britain and was coined by Beatrice Potter as evident from her book 'The Co-operative Movement' in 1891 and 'Industrial Democracy' in 1897, where it was regarded as the alternative to individual bargaining.

In India, however, collective bargaining is a late development and has marked its presence only in the year 1918, in Ahmedabad.

Voluntary collective bargaining in industry and commerce has developed in India since independence.

The textile industry in Ahmedabad has the longest history of settlement of disputes by mutual negotiation and voluntary arbitration can claim to have paved the way towards modern collective bargaining although the experiment at Ahmedabad was not directly followed elsewhere.

The inspiration of peaceful settlement of differences between management and labour at Ahmedabad came from Gandhiji, who set out his philosophy of industrial relations in his autobiography.

In 1918, Gandhiji was leading the textile workers of Ahmedabad in their demand for better working conditions, but even though he had supported their strike, he was advocating the resolution of conflict by negotiation and mutual discussion between the accredited organisations of labourers and employers. Where negotiation failed the recommended conciliation, he suggested reference to an agreed arbitrator or board of arbitrators whose decision would be binding. In 1918, when the wage disputes were eventually settled, at Gandhiji's intervention by reference to an arbitration board representing both employers and workers he declared that he did not see why all future difference should not be settled in the same way.

Gandhiji was successful in bringing the Ahmedabad Mill Owners' Association round to his point of view and in 1920 it was agreed that any dispute or difference of opinion which the workplace could not themselves settle should be referred to Gandhiji and Seth Mangal Das, the President of Association, as arbitrators. In case they could not reach agreement, provision was made for reference to an umpire whose award would be final.

This system prevailed until 1939 in Ahmedabad. The system of voluntary arbitration could hardly be called collective bargaining. Usually they were able to reach agreement, but on several occasions they had to recourse to an umpire on some unresolved points. In the first 16 months of its existence the Board gave 23 awards but not all the questions which came before it were the subject of actual disputes.

Just before the second World War the system of arbitration at Ahmedabad seemed to be breaking down and in 1940, under war time conditions, a reference was made to compulsory adjudication under the Bombay Industrial Regulation Act, 1946.

In 1952, after a lapse of about 14 years, the Ahmedabad Mill Owners' Association and the Textile Labour Union signed two agreements, initially for two years, by which the machinery of voluntary arbitration was revived. This was a proper collective bargaining between the two representative organisations, who agreed that in future all disputes between mills and their employees should be settled out of court.

Collective Bargaining in Ahmedabad textile industry is now carried on at two levels, viz-

    a. between Mill Owners' Association and Textile Labour Association and

    b. between individual mills and Textile Labour Association.

In 1955, a general agreement on the subject of annual bonus was reached for the years 1953-57, covering all the mills. In 1957, a joint productivity council was set up for Ahmedabad textiles.

From the above discussion, it is clear that a continuing collective bargaining process has come into being in Ahmedabad textile industry.

There was, however, another early instance of an employers' association and an industrial union coming together to solve their problems. This was in the Coir industry in Travancore (Kerala). However, both in Ahmedabad and Kerala, collective bargaining process was for group of employers.

The earliest example of collective bargaining within individual concern was that of Joint Steamer Companies in Calcutta. Their first written agreement with Bengal Mariners Union was in the year 1946. Among the manufacturing enterprises the earliest record of the post-war collective agreements was made by Dunlop Rubber Company at Shagunge in West Bengal in 1947. The Bata Shoe Company in West Bengal made its first agreement in 1948. In 1951, Indian Aluminium Company, in1952, the Imperial Tobacco Company, in 1953, the Mysore Iron and Steel Company, in 1955 TISCO, Jamshedpur, in 1956, National Newsprint and Paper Mills at Nepanagar (M.P.) have signed their collective agreements with their workmen.

From the above discussions, it is, therefore, clear that from 1950 onwards collective bargaining has acquired importance in India. The new industry groups, Engineering, Chemicals, etc. with a higher degree of professionalisation in management have developed collective bargaining as an institution. In India, collective bargaining is taking place at various levels, viz. Plant level, Industry level and National level. We have illustrated above certain plant level and industry level Collective Bargaining Agreements in the past. The agreements at the national level are generally bipartite agreements and are finalised at conferences of labour and managements convened by the Governement of India. The Delhi Agreement of 7th February, 1951 and Bonus Agreement for Plantation workers of January, 1956 are examples of such bipartite agreements in the past.

The issues of bargaining in India are generally wages, dearness allowance, retirement benefits, bonus, annual leave, casual leave, paid holidays, etc. Study of Employers' Federation of India shows that 'wages' issue is most prominent among others. Information about collective bargaining settlement, compiled by Labour Bureau, Shimla for the quarter ending December, 1994 shows that 115 settlements have been arrived through Collective Bargaining Agreements during the period in India. Out of these, only one settlement relates to the State sphere while 114 fall in the Centre sphere. We have illustrated the position in the following Table.

Month-wise Collective Bargaining Agreements during the quarter ending 31st December, 1994

Sl. Subject	Number of Agreements						Total	
	Oct. 1994		Nov. 1994		Dec. 1994			
	C.S.	S.S	C.S	S.S	C.S	S.S	C.S.	S.S
1. Wages/DA	09	-	13	-	05	-	27	-
2. Bonus	17	-	11	-	02	-	30	-
3. Overtime	02	-	02	-	02	-	06	-
4. House Rent	04	-	04	-	-	-	08	-
5. Health	01	-	02	-	01	-	04	-
6. Welfare	01	-	04	-	02	-	07	-
7. Hours of Work	02	-	-	-	-	-	02	-
8. Conveyance	03	-	02	-	-	-	05	-
9. Leave	04	-	03	-	02	-	09	-
10. Liveries	04	-	06	-	-	-	10	-
11. Service matter	32	01	20	-	19	-	71	01
12. Others	07	-	09	-	01	-	17	-
Total	48	01	09	-	23	-	114	01

Politicisation of trade unions, failure of both parties to devote adequate time, third party intervention, etc. are some of the problems of collective bargaining in India. Mary Parker Follet criticised the collective bargaining process particularly for absence of workers' rights and privileges which itself stand against their bargaining power. Workers being weak bargainers, can never expect to gain from collective bargaining process.

REVIEW QUESTIONS

1. Define Collective Bargaining. What are its important characteristics and what are the important pre-requisites of its success?

2. Considering Indian industrial environment, do you think, Collective Bargaining Process is at all helpful to sustain good worker-management relations?

3. Make a review of Collective Bargaining scenario in India.

4. To make Collective Bargaining Process a success, what are the roles of workers and management representatives.

CHAPTER
13 LABOUR ECONOMICS AND LABOUR INSTITUTIONS

LEARNING OBJECTIVES

This chapter explains in detail:

☐ the concept of labour markets, trade unions and labour institutions in India

☐ the effects of unemloyment and balance of payment problems

☐ technology upgradation and employment in India

☐ people engaged in agricultural activities in India

☐ absenteeism and labour turnover

CONTENT OUTLINE

13.1 INTRODUCTION

Labour Economics studies the demand and supply for the important factor of production, i.e. human beings. Marshall and Smith are the two pioneering economists who first recognised that the study of market for labour is not possible without understanding the social relations of production, long-term contractual arrangement, problems of motivation, institutions like unions and internal labour markets, etc. All these characteristic requirements differentiate the market for labour from other markets.

The most important development in the modern Labour Economics is the development of the concept of Human Capital. Human capital analyses individual decision making in regard to supply of labour and other behavioural areas which are more related with sociology rather than economics. Before the development of the concept of human capital, labour supply decisions were considered more as an economic rationality. By making such decision as an inter-relational variable of education, skill, investment, wages, working hours, etc. the subject of labour economics has been demarcated from the traditional economic analysis.

Like labour supply, which emphasise on individual decision making, as an outcome of different inter-relational variables, labour demand and firms behaviour is influenced by internal labour markets, hiring, promotion, wage policies and the structure of wages in various markets, etc. Most of the firms maintain computerised personnel records to analyse their demand for labour. There are many techniques for analysis of labour demand. There are many techniques for analysis of labour demand. For example, a firm may study the likely response of workers to a particular wage and personnel policy (which optimises their profits). Some firms offer maximum compensation to match with the workers' expectations and then try to maximise the utility of workers, while others study the effect of deferred compensation, piece rates and other systems of rewards. The Neo-classical model on study of labour demand examines the magnitude of elasticities and cross-elasticities of labour demand for workers of different skills and the effect of minimum wages on employment. Similarly, elasticities of substitution and complementarity are also studied to analyse the labour demand.

In the area of labour institutions, effects of unions on wages, wages in unionised and non-unionised industries and occupations, differences between union and non-union workers, etc. are studied. We have separately discussed the labour institutions/trade unions in India.

13.2 LABOUR MARKETS

Demand, supply and institutions interact in labour markets and labour economics studies the operation of labour markets considering all these issues. Analysis of labour markets are carried out for different occupational segments, viz., markets for blue-collar workers, markets for white-collar workers, markets for professionals, etc. Investigating markets for knowledgeable and skilled workers, differentiating supply and demand forces in the markets, geographic and industrial mobilities, unemployment, wage pattern, etc. are the areas for studying the labour markets. Recently, however, macro changes in wages and unemployment over a given period of time, both within the country and across countries, are also studied to synthesize the facts of the labour markets with the basic principles of economics.

In India, pioneering studies in labour economics are institutionally being carried out by the Indian Society of Labour Economics (ISLE). ISLE organises national level conferences on different areas of labour economics and try to develop this as a distinct discipline having importance both in the academic and professional research in understanding the trend of the most important factors of production, i.e. human beings. ISLE regularly publishes Indian Journal of Labour Economics, which is considered as an international journal on the subject of Labour Economics. Most of the studies are now being carried out at micro/unit level. Macro level studies even though are there, for obvious paucity of labour statistics, much success is yet to be achieved in this respect.

13.3 TRADE UNIONS AND LABOUR INSTITUTIONS IN INDIA

Trade Unions are voluntary organisations of workers. Through joint action, they protect and promote the interest of workers. With the setting up of large-scale industrial units, a new class of workers, dependent solely on wages for their livelihood, have emerged in India. In the absence of collective action, this working class had to be content with wages, which they could individually negotiate with the employers. In such a circumstance, individual workers had virtually no bargaining power, perhaps for reasons of abundant supply of labour. Hence, the need for joint action at least to sustain, if not to improve, their bargaining power against the employers had been strongly felt. The pace of such action had been accentuated with the recognition by the community to form unions to institutionalise workers' rights to organise, to press for their demand collectively and to go for strike when their claims are not accepted.

13.3.1 History

The earliest known Trade unions in India are:

(i)   The Bombay Millhands' Association, formed in 1890 for the purpose of urging the government for improvements in factory law. However, it soon became defunct after the passing of the 1891 Act.

(ii)   The Amalgamated Society of Railway Servants of India and Burma formed in 1897 by Anglo-Indians and domiciled Europeans employed on railways. This, however was more of a friendly association than to secure concessions.

(iii) Printers' Union started in Calcutta in 1905.

(iv)   The Bombay postal union formed in 1907.

(v)   The Kamgar Hitwardhak Sabha, Mumbai in 1910. This was a body of social workers and not workers of the organisation. They were interested in general welfare of labour.

In the decade following the end of First World War, we have witnessed in India rapid developments in the field of trade unionism. These were the beginning of the Trade Union Movement in India. Within a period of five years (1919-1923) large number of unions were formed in different parts of the country. The movement initially had made an inroad in the Railways, in Postal and Telegraph Departments, among seamen and in the Textile Industry in Ahmedabad city and also in some other centres.

Although individual unions were well accepted by the society almost since their stage of formation, employers in majority of the cases refused to recognise the unions on the plea that union executives consisted of outsiders. Workers interested in trade union activities were victimised by the employers. To thwart Trade Union Movement, the then employers succeeded to get an amendment passed in the Indian Penal Code in 1913, declaring Trade Unions as illegal bodies. The Buckingham & Carnatic Mills case of 1921 in Madras High Court, granting an interim injunction against the Madras Labour Union, further added to this fuel. At this point of time Trade Union leaders suddenly found that they are liable to prosecution and imprisonment even for bonafide trade union activities. In March, 1921, the legislative assembly of the Government of India, on the motion of Late N.M. Joshi, the then General Secretary of the All India Trade Union Congress (AITUC), passed a resolution for the registration and protection of Trade Unions. Since then, the pace of the Indian Trade Union Movement continued unabatingly and reached its height during 1928-29, when communists wooed the world of Indian Labour.

After World War II and independence of the country in 1947, political considerations led to the division of Trade Union leadership. In 1947, Indian National Trade Union Congress (INTUC) was formed. The differences with the socialist workers inside AITUC, led to the formation of Hind Mazdoor Sabha and subsequently to the Central Indian Trade Union Congress (CITU), representing leftist. The socialists under the leadership of Dr Ram Manohar Lohia formed the Hind Mazdoor Panchayat and the Jan Sangh set up the Bhartiya Mazdoor Sangh. Since then four more Central Trade Union Organisations have been formed to accelerate the pace of Indian Trade Union Movement.

Trade unions in India are associated mainly with the two international trade union federations, viz., the World Federation of Trade Unions (WFTU) and the International Confederation of Free Trade Unions (WFTU).

In matters of industrial relations and workers' productivity, trade unions play crucial role. Relative strength of any particular union is determined from its membership details.

In the Table below, we have furnished verified membership details of ten major Central Trade Unions in India.

Organisations	No. of Unions	Membership (in lakhs)	Percentage
INTUC	1604	22.36	36.5
BMS	1333	12.11	19.8
HMS	426	7.63	12.5
UTUC (L.S.)	134	6.21	10.1
NLD	172	2.47	4.0
UTUC	175	1.66	2.7
TUCC	65	1.23	2.0
NFITU	80	0.84	1.4
AITUC	1080	3.45	5.6
CITU	1474	3.31	5.4
Total	6543	61.27	100.00

Source : Different issues of Indian Labour Journal

In a very recently concluded survey, it has been indicated that BMS is having the highest membership followed by INTUC, CITU, HMS and AITUC. The latest membership details of the above five major Central Trade Union Organisations are presented below:

Organisation	Membership Claimed	Membership verified
INTUC	54,35,705	25,87,378
AITUC	29,73,933	9,05,975
HMS	43,56,034	13,18,804
CITU	23,86,242	17,68,044
BMS	40,81,424	27,69,556

Source: Business India, August 29 - September 11, 1994

To authenticate the membership claim of different trade union organisations, government is now urging the employers to affect deduction of membership fees from the pay of those employees who give such instruction in writing to them. Fees, thus, collected will then be diverted to the respective trade union organisations.

Beginning from 1928-29 till 1970s, trade unions in India reached a commanding height. Almost all public sector units and major private sector organisations by this time have been unionised. However, since early 1980s we have seen the declining phase of trade unions in India. In fact from this period onwards industrial restructuring process began in India.

With the announcement of new economic policy of the Government of India in 1991, labour institutions and trade unions in India are now facing a challenging task ahead. The new economic policy poses following challenges to the trade unions:

1. Gradual shift of employment from the organised sector to unorganised sector. Out of the total labour force of 317 million in the country, the organised sector employs merely 26.8 million, i.e., only 8.5 per cent. Such shift in employment is a major phenomenal trend during post industrial restructuring process (began in 1980s). This trend obviously gives employers of the unorganised sector the advantage to flout labour laws.

2. The increasing emphasis on exports and emergence of free exporting processing zones in different parts of the country is again a major source of threat to the trade unions as such units are also getting the advantage to immune them from labour laws.

3. The growth of employment over the last few years has severely affected industrial restructuring process. Added to this is the burden of huge number of unemployment as nearly four million people from organised sector are likely to lose their employment in the process of structural adjustment programme.

4. Closure of sick industrial units which employ 45 lakh people, sooner or later, will further add to the burden of unemployment. Government of India even though initiated to provide safety net under Voluntary Retirement Scheme (VRS) to give some benefits to the workers thus losing their jobs, in reality, is yet to come out with any concrete proposal (excepting mooting of the idea). In a national level seminar organised by the Indian Society of Labour Economics

during 1992, the Department of Industries closely circulated a paper on proposed VRS, giving the details of the government's resolution on such count taken during February, 1992. However, the said scheme is yet to be operationalised.

5. To keep pace with the global competition accentuated by the market globalisation programme (an outcome of economic liberalisation policy), Indian industries are now required to introduce new technology. In industrial units conventional machines are now being replaced by Numerically Controlled (NC), Computer Numerally Controlled (CNC), Direct Numerically Controlled (DNC) Machines, Flexible Manufacturing System (FMS), etc. Such introduction of new technology is now making the traditional skills redundant, which necessitates redeployment of the workers after suitable retraining or to replace the workers (who cannot be retrained) by the new working force. This new working force being educated and skilled is mostly inducted in managerial or supervisory grades, resulting in reduction in employment of workers. In addition, new technology being more systematic is enabling the management to have greater control over the labour process. All these, therefore, severely erode the powers of the unions.

It is evident from the analysis of industrial dispute figures over the last few years that lockouts are responsible for more number of loss of man-days. This clearly indicates the reduced power of unions to influence the employment relations in the industrial units. The fact that the trade unions are losing their powers is evident from the fact that in many units, enterprise level unions are emerging. Such enterprise level unions are internal or independent unions having no political affiliation. Hence, in the context of the present scenario, it is expected that trade unions in India will have to make them more transparent and responsible to survive in the coming years.

13.4 THE THEORY OF EMPLOYMENT / UNEMPLOYMENT

13.4.1 Importance of Unemployment and balance of payment problems

Ever-since it started developing on a planned basis (since 1950-51), Indian economy is ailing from certain chronic economic problems. Among these problems, unemployment and rising balance of payment crisis have assumed critical proportions, especially since 1970. Without solving these two problems or at least reducing the acuteness of these problems, the Government of India or the Planning Commission cannot pay attention to the other more general problems. When unemployment is confined to only a section of the rural population, government can give some dole to pacify the unemployed. But when the urban population also becomes unemployed to a substantial extent and particularly when they are educated unemployed, it becomes difficult to contain the situation; the situation becomes grave. Similarly, when the balance of payments deficit remains within reasonable proportion, government can pay attention to other internal problems. When the deficits increase over time, government has to borrow from agencies as India has drawn from IMF or government can see no way of either reducing the deficits or to find means for paying back the foreign money. Moreover, indebtedness creates psychological phobia both in the Government and among the people whom the government serves. Therefore, the question of indebtedness gets top priority in the thinking of planners, policy makers and economists. There is an inherent difficulty in the situation. The problems of unemployment and balance of payment deficits cannot be taken up separately. It must be tackled together. Inter dependence between the level of employment and the extent of deficit is such that if the Government takes a policy of reducing unemployment, deficit is likely to increase (as they are inversely related).

13.4.2 Interrelation Between Unemployment and Balance of Payment Deficit

Let us now consider the following simple Keynesian income generation model.

Let National Income be denoted by 'Y' (a variable), C = Consumption depending on 'Y' is also a variable. I = Investment (autonomous and given). Investment is unpredictable because it is influenced by investors' behaviour. X = Exports of the country also autonomous and given (depends on foreigners' demands for our goods). M = Imports, a variable depending on Y, a part of the total consumption of goods by countrymen.

Then $Y = C + I + X - M$

Since I and X are constants we use bars on them. 'Y' or national income is measured as the total value of domestic outputs of final goods. Outputs of intermediate goods and raw materials are embodied in the calculation of final goods output. To avoid double counting, such outputs of intermediate goods and raw materials are not separately added again.

Thus, output of final goods consists of total consumption by the people of domestic goods, total investment, i.e. total purchase of machinery and any exports that have taken place out of the domestic output. All final goods, therefore, can be presented as below:

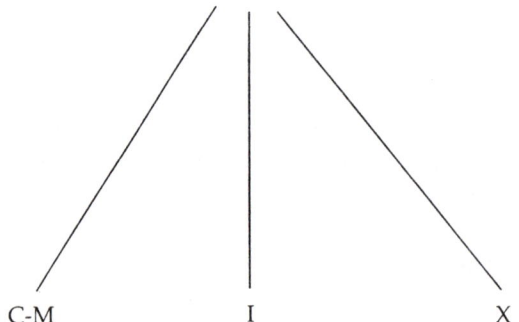

$$C-M \qquad I \qquad X$$

C - M = Consumption of domestic goods

In the above presentation, we have assumed that imports consists of only consumables, alternatively if there is some import of machinery that has been included in I (Investment), then such imports are also subtracted and the total subtraction is again M (Imports) Now we can write final goods produced:

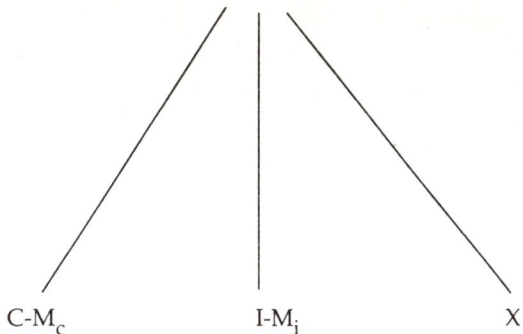

C - Mc = Consumption of domestic goods

I - Mi = Investment of domestic machinery

X = Exports

Mc = Import of consumables

Mi = Import of investment

Entire M = (Mc + Mi) to be subtracted.

National output (finished goods) = National Income.

$Y = C + I + X - M$

C = Consumption of domestic goods and imports

I = Investment of domestic machinery and imported machinery

X = Exports

M = Subtract Imported Consumption and Investment from C + I

When the national output produced (Y) and spent for consumption, investment and exports cannot employ even a reasonable part of the country's resources, we say that there is imbalance in the economy. This imbalance is an 'internal imbalance', i.e. an imbalance on the domestic front. On the other hand when there is an inequality between exports and imports, especially when import exceeds export, we say that there is an external imbalance or an imbalance on the external front.

In other words unemployment signifies a lack of internal balance and the balance of trade deficit (M - X) gives an external balance.

13.4.3 Inter-relationship Creates Problems For Policy Decision

In India, we are facing today, a combination of internal and external imbalances. This creates a special difficulty because the policy that government takes to remove internal imbalance usually acts counter to policies designed at removing external deficit. For example, government expenditure to increase C & I through road construction and other kinds of short-term investment, even flood-relief, food for work programmes and the usual social benefit measures increase national output and level of employment. However, out of the new incomes created by these schemes a part go to increase income further in the hands of businessmen who sell the consumption and investment goods. With the extra incomes the businessmen in turn buy goods partly from the domestic market and partly from foreign market. Now there is already a deficit in the Balance of trade X - M < 0 (negative). Now M rising and X stagnating, the balance of trade deficit or the imbalance on the external front worsens as a result of policies aiming at reducing unemployment.

In short unemployment cannot be reduced without raising incomes, a part of which must go to rich people also through increased business and imports tend to rise even if by a small amount. There is nothing in the mechanism that can close or improve the deficit on the external front.

The major difficulty in taking anti-unemployment policy is, therefore, an existence of an external deficit which tends to get worse when income and employment increase. The standard fiscal (budgetary) and monetary (RBI's) methods are designed to boost the overall level of activity in a country so that both employment and national income increase. These methods are called the macro-economic methods of raising employment. As we have seen, the existence of an external deficit in India discourages to some extent the macro-economic income raising policies taken up by the government.

There are, however, other methods of raising employment which are less harmful to the external balance. If a given output is produced by a labour intensive method rather than by an automatic and capital intensive technique, then the likelihood of increased business income and the resultant import diminishes. In the diagram, we have curved the various alternative methods of producing a fixed output. The equal output curve is called an iso-quant because output remains fixed as we move along the curve.

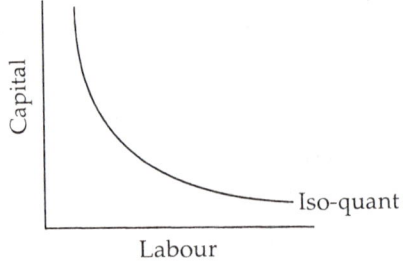

As we go down less and less capital is used, more and more labour is used in substitution for capital and output neither increases nor diminishes. Clearly there is not one iso-quant but many iso-quants for various levels of output. At each level of output the capital-labour substitution possibilities are shown by one curve (and at another level of output by another curve).

If employment is raised through substitution of labour for capital without raising the output then the multiplier effect on national income may not operate strongly. Furthermore, though wage incomes increase, the owners of capital may receive less because less capital is used and it is not likely that imports should increase and balance of trade deficit should get worse.

We have seen that the first micro economic cause of continued unemployment problem in India is a wrong choice of the technique of production, where labour can be substituted for capital without loss of efficiency, the businessmen should be induced to make such substitution. Left to themselves, the owners of the firms do not always make such substitution because they are concerned about their own profits rather than the overall level of employment in the country. If the government takes a tax-cum-subsidy policy on the use of labour, wherever possible, then labour intensive techniques will be used by the producers. The tax-cum-subsidy policy will be designed to increase the effective price of capital by tax and to reduce the effective price of labour by a subsidy financed by the proceeds of tax.

The second cause for continued unemployment, also microeconomic in nature, is the changing product-mix in the country. With the industrialisation, there is a natural tendency for employment to increase rapidly in all sectors. All industries grow, though at various rates and each industry employs more labour than before. The overall level of employment, therefore, should increase at a reasonably good rate.

In our country, however, the growth of national income is not accompanied by a satisfactory rate of growth in employment. The reasons for such decline in employment are:

(i) Composition of the industrial production may have changed and new composition may have proportionately less employment potential than the previous composition.

(ii) Within an industry, technology may have changed and technology with much less employment potential may be much more common now than before.

The particular product-mix to be manufactured, at both inter-industry and intra-industry levels, is clearly a critical determinant of the employment implications of any industrialisation strategy.

The composition of output at the industry level is determined to a large extent by the structure of aggregate demand, that is, by the demands of domestic consumers, foreigners, the government and the private investors.

Intra-industry product choice is based on classification of products in three ways:

(i) Cross-elasticities of demand (in case of identical products);

(ii) Grouping products by physical attributes;

(iii) Classification as per characteristics.

After deciding which goods should be produced or more realistically, in conjunction with that decision, a decision still has to be made as to how they are to be produced, with what technology and factor proportions.

Appropriate technology may be defined as the set of techniques, which makes optimum use of available resources in a given environment. Detailed product-by-product studies are the surest way of estimating the extent to which the adoption of more appropriate techniques can be expected to increase labour use. At least this should not be forgotten that as long as the marginal productivity of labour is positive, every increase in employment increases the productivity of capital and, therefore, increasing employment always raises output.

The concept of labour intensity is used in three senses:

(i) Share of labour input in the total value of output;

(ii) Wages as percentage of the value added;

(iii) Employment component of productive capital or of output.

The rates of substitution between capital and labour are different in different industries and are different at different levels of output. Let us now consider the technology equilibrium below:

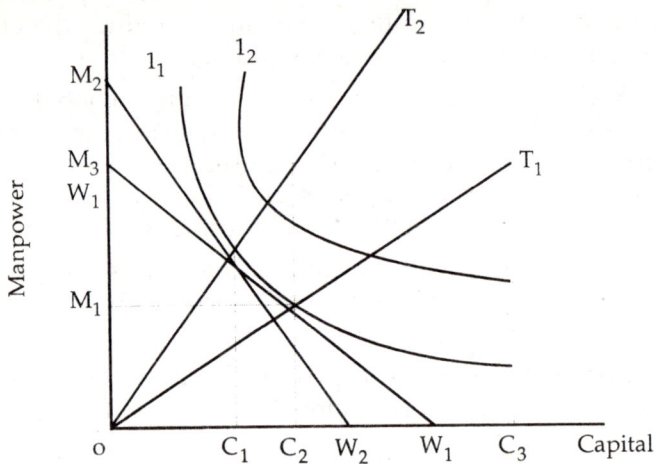

I_1, I_2 are different iso-quants for different levels of production. The entrepreneurs would be indifferent to the factor-mix at each of these curves but he would always try to move on to the higher curve so long as economics of scale will allow. The actual decision about the level of production would be guided by technological possibilities and factor endowments. On iso-quant I_1, all points, such as a, b, c are of equal significance to the entrepreneur, but the alternative technologies may not be available on all of them. If only two technologies, namely, OT_1 and OT_2 are feasible, then considering X axis to represent capital and Y axis manpower, OT_1, would be a capital intensive technology, whereas OT_2 would be a labour intensive technology. Suppose OC_2 is the investible capital resource available in the economy under technology OT_1 then only OM_1 amount of manpower could be employed. In case OM_3 represents the available manpower in the community, then M_1 - M_3 would be the quantum of unemployment. To provide full employment, technology OT_2 may be useful, but in this case only OC_1 amount of capital would be required, which implies that C_1 C_2, the surplus capital resource, may depress the rate of interest thus making substitution of labour more plausible. For obtaining full employment with OT_1, the amount of capital required would be OC_3, indicating the need for additional amount of capital represented by the difference C_2 C_3. The decision to change from technology OT_1 to technology OT_2 would require much capital judgement on economic parameters and considerable administrative reorganisation. Such changes to be stable and effective will have to be supported by technical training, managerial improvement, appropriate fabricating equipment, better entrepreneurial motivation and the workers' adoption to the new production organisation; restraint on militant trade unionism, changes in labour laws, readjustment in rates of interest and wage and elimination of artificial support to one factor against another will also be essential. Much political overtones are in-built in these considerations, which make the decision very sensitive to various non-economic influences.

The third reason for unemployment is macro-economic in nature. J.M. Keynes, in 1930, brought into economics the concept of lacking effective demand. Instead of the demand for one commodity falling because of arrival of the substitute commodities in the market there may be a fall in demand for all commodities at a time. This happens at the turn of a business cycle. After a period of boom a pin point is reached when business activity is at its highest. Immediately after this, the level of activity takes a downward turn and the process becomes cumulative when everyone starts reducing output on a speculative spree. It is true that an actual fall in effective demand was a feature of mature capitalist countries only (during the 1930s there was a wide spread slump in business activity in all the capitalist countries in the world). It is possible even in an underdeveloped country that effective demand should become stagnant after a boom period. The industrialists of our country very often suggest that such has been the case in India ever since the late second half of 1960s.

We have introduced the concept of macro economic concept or general lack of effective demand was a feature of the capitalist countries of the world during the great depression of 1930s. However, after an overshooting of investment activity or a boom in business there sometimes follows a short recessionary period even in a developing country. With the inception of second five year plan of India, the government laid some emphasis on building up a good industrial base for a self-sustained growth of the country. As a result during the first half of the 1960s an over expansion of capacity occurred in some industries mainly the capital goods industries on which the second plan laid special/particular stress. In the later half of 1960s these industrialists were faced with insufficient demand relative to the capacity of production. A general recession in all capital goods industries set in. In this manner at a very early stage of development the Indian business community was faced with what is usually a feature of mature capitalist countries alone. During the 1970s there was some revival from the recession even in the capital goods industries. The consumer goods industries on the other hand were faced with a different kind of demand problem. The prices fixed for many durable consumer goods are such that even in a vast country like India, there cannot be much demand for these goods. The demand comes from an exclusive class of people which have very few members.

Capacity under-utilisation may also be attributed to an important economic cause for unemployment in India. Capacity under-utilisation has increased from 20 per cent to 30 per cent during the fourth plan period alone. Labour unrest, material shortages, transport bottlenecks, power failures, managerial shortcomings, shortage of demand, ambitious project planning, etc. may be held responsible for capacity under-utilisation. Apart from these, structural characteristics of the Indian industries, i.e. monopoly, oligopoly structure may also be held responsible for wide spread unemployment. Monopolists restrict their output to reach high profits in the protected market.

The above being the main causes of unemployment in India, the appropriate policies for reducing unemployment should be as follows:

(i)   The first and foremost cause was a wrong choice of technique of production. The government policy should be a combination of subsidy and tax to favour the labour intensive method of production in preference to an equally efficient capital intensive one.

(ii) The second cause is the development of a product-mix in which the weight of those goods is increasing which are naturally less labour intensive than the industries which they are replacing. The government policy under plan perspective should be based on a comparison between two different goals of increasing national income and increasing employment. If it is considered that reducing unemployment is more important than national income then some of the highly productive modern industries should be given disincentives and traditional labour intensive industries should receive encouragement from the government. This can also be done by means of taxes and subsidies selectively applied.

(iii) The third or macro economic cause is more difficult to cure. In this case a tax-cum-subsidy method will not work because there exists a general lack of demand not for selected industries which can be helped by the government but for many industries at a time. One method of tackling this problem is a redistribution of income in favour of those people whose propensity to save is high and away from those whose propensity to save is low. From the circular flow of income and demand for goods the saved parts of income are withdrawn. If income is redistributed in favour of those who save less and consume more then the withdrawn part diminishes and most of the income flows back to the industrialists in the form of fresh demand for goods and as a result new employment is created. This situation is for generating mass incomes, which create demand for commodities consumed by the common people, for example, coarse clothes, bulk drugs, commercial vehicles, railway wagons, buses, cheap radios, bicycles, electronic gadgets, etc. and the unemployment can be substantially reduced by means of mass production of these commodities. The erstwhile socialist countries, in spite of similar problems as we are facing, have made good progress in increasing the level of employment by keeping income distribution fair. Their recent political change-over, however, aggravated the problem of unemployment.

Table No - 1

No. of units effecting Lay off and workers Laid off by different causes during 1987-1992

Cause	1987		1988		1989		1990		1991		1992	
	Units	Workers	Units	Workers	Units	Workers	Units	Workers	Units	Workers	Units	Workers
Shortage of power	333	100593	225	60727	206	41283	178	35933	131	28661	166	60187
Shortage of raw material	128	14533	123	15856	141	13076	107	8246	127	18854	72	12882
Breakwown of machinery	47	4246	35	4466	31	2882	27	1576	29	3577	40	6221
Lack of demand	113	8800	103	3859	76	2929	63	1817	82	3157	60	2391
Financial stringency	35	8524	38	6025	36	3973	24	2771	36	2235	16	3973
Off season	0	0	1	78	1	19	1	10	0	0	0	0
Others	53	8229	52	14098	47	6491	42	13718	56	14576	54	10261
Total	709	144925	577	105109	538	70653	442	64080	461	71060	408	95915

Source: Labour Bureau, Shimla

Table No - 2

Cause-wise number of units effecting retrenchment and workers retrenched during 1987 - 1992

	1987		1988		1989 (P)		1990 (P)		1991 (P)		1992 (P)	
	U	W	U	W	U	W	U	W	U	W	U	W
Financial Stringency	50	618	60	687	32	529	77	958	40	611	29	1632
Shortage of raw materials	21	470	17	320	14	192	14	318	11	173	4	83
Shortage of power	2	29	2	237	3	20	2	16	0	0	1	16
Breakdown of machinery	0	0	1	33	1	13	0	0	2	9	1	10
Lack of demand	149	1210	186	1957	69	518	100	1073	100	1345	97	810
Off Season	2	42	0	0	0	0	1	2	0	0	0	0
Others	103	2566	101	1607	50	1962	69	615	69	2035	40	711
Not known	29	267	12	173	5	24	5	55	13	223	3	16
Total	356	5202	379	5014	174	3258	268	3037	235	4369	175	3338

Source: Labour Bureau, Shimla.

Notes : U = Units, W = Workers, P = Provisional.

Data of 1992 is from January - November.

Table No - 3

Distribution of Strikes and Lockouts by different causes during 1987-1992

Causes	1987		1988		1989		1990 (P)		1991 (P)		1992 (P)	
	S	L	S	L	S	L	S	L	S	L	S	L
Wages and allowances	423	61	413	60	391	34	406	36	367	68	167	44
Bonus	94	41	83	34	92	16	64	8	58	12	9	10
Personnel	209	27	202	27	274	26	225	11	212	58	65	29
Retrenchment	61	3	58	1	36	3	46	8	35	4	9	3
Leave & hours of work	18	4	17	11	18	3	26	1	50	2	5	9
Indiscipline and violence	62	184	72	196	100	175	114	171	111	223	29	165
Others	447	122	424	101	446	112	552	107	456	151	192	96
Not known	34	9	35	11	40	20	30	24	24	40	11	8

Source : Labour Bureau, Shimla.

Notes: S = Strikes, L = Lockouts, P = Provisional 1992 data is upto November.

13.5 PRESENT SCENARIO OF EMPLOYMENT AND UNEMPLOYMENT IN INDIA

Unemployment affects all groups of people in general and young and middle aged persons in particular. The most widely acceptable definition of unemployment refers "to some one (person) who has been taken as such (unemployed) after having applied unsuccessfully for a job and who having registered with a government agency, responsible either for finding jobs or for obtaining financial aid, still finds no work". In economic sense employment is defined as freelance or salaried activity aimed at production for a market.

In India, unemployment is measured by various methods using different concepts. The most conventional method is to consider those persons as unemployed who are idling involuntarily, i.e. these persons are available and willing to work but are not able to find any work. There are different types of unemployment which can be listed as follows:

1.   Mass unemployment

2.   Structural unemployment

3.   Frictional unemployment

4.   Seasonal unemployment and

5.   Residual unemployment

Mass unemployment is a general phenomena in any developing country. The problem, however, is more acute in under developed countries. The reason for mass unemployment is general imbalance in economic activity which renders a large number of population unemployed.

Structural unemployment is for shift in employment pattern from one sector of economic activity to another. For example, in recent times in India this type of unemployment in agricultural and rural industries is evident, resulting a major shift in employment from agriculture to other sectors of the economy, similarly from manufacturing sector a large chunk of employment shift is now taking place to tertiary sector which by now is the highest contributor to net domestic product.

Frictional unemployment is primarily for reasons of technological change. In many areas of economic activity there is a trend to substitute capital for labour by introducing technology efficient system. Very recently this type of unemployment is evident in Indian industries which have now gone for major technological change. In agriculture also unemployment is rising partly for substitution of labour by capital, i.e. for use of technology efficient system.

Seasonal unemployment is a common phenomenon both in Indian agriculture and industries. For part of the year, huge number of working population becomes jobless.

Residual unemployment indicates the remaining nature of unemployment, which is not classifiable under above categories. Mostly under this head we categorise that type of unemployment which are caused generally for the failure of job seekers either for not acquiring the requisite skill or for not having the physical fitness to work. In reality people categorised under this head are unemployable.

13.5.1 Backlog of Unemployment

Even though growth of the economy leads to more employment in India but because of the mismatch between creation of employment (demand) and addition to labour force (supply), we are witnessing higher and higher backlog of unemployment at the end of each five-year plan. The backlog of unemployment in 15-59 age group at the beginning of the sixth and seventh plan was 11.31 millions and 7.84 millions respectively and at the end of the same plan was 7.84 and 3.75 millions respectively. As a percentage of labour force, backlog of unemployment accounted for 2.9 per cent and 1.2 per cent respectively. The current figure of unemployment is approximately 13.09 million. The mismatch between increase in employment (2 per cent per annum average) and addition to labour force (2.5 to 3 per cent) in seventies and eighties resulted in the rise of backlog of unemployment. The estimates of backlog of unemployment, as per the Employment Exchange statistics, however, are much higher. This is presumably for two reasons– all the registrants are not unemployed and all the employed do not register themselves.

The labour force is projected to increase by about 35 million between 1992-1997 (eighth plan) and another 36 million during 1997-2002. The total persons, therefore, to be provided employment are estimated at 58 million during 1990-1995 and 94 million in a decade, i.e. 1992-2002. Hence, to achieve full employment goal in India by the end of Eighth Plan and by 2000 A.D. employment growth per year has to be 4 per cent and 3 per cent respectively.

13.5.2 Educated Unemployment

According to NSS Data, 47 per cent of men and 63 per cent of women unemployed in urban area are matriculates or graduates. For the rural unemployed the corresponding percentage figures are 43 and 24 respectively. For obvious political clout and wastage of resources, this class of unemployed receives more attention than others. However, their problem of employability is perhaps related to quality of education and skills. Many schemes of the government to make the educated employable (vocational guidance, training and apprenticeship) have not yielded any fruitful results. Different self employment schemes to adjust this unemployed, however, is one positive step which belatedly started yielding results. At governmental level different infrastructural facilities like loans, machinery, skills, electricity, markets, etc. are being provided to ensure gainful self-employment to this class of unemployed.

13.5.3 Economic Liberalization and the Problem of Unemployment

The process of economic liberalisation, which began since July, 1991 is expected to throw out a significant percentage of workforce from employment. Thus, additional unemployment of 1 to 3 million during 1992-93 and 4.8 million in 1993-94 (both in public and private sector) is expected to add to the problem of unemployment as a consequential effect of economic liberalisation programme. To ensure redeployment of such employees through training (where possible) or to give benefits by offering exit incentive (where workers cannot be trained and redeployed), Government of India has set up National Renewal Fund (NRF). The objectives of NRF can be enumerated as follows:

1. To provide assistance to cover the costs of retraining and redeployment of employees arising as a result of modernisation, technology upgradation and industrial restructuring.

2. To provide funds, where, necessary for compensation of employees affected by restructuring or closure of industrial units, both in the public and private sectors.

3. To provide funds for employment generation schemes both in the organised and unorganised sectors in order to provide a social safety net for labour needs arising from the consequences of industrial restructuring.

13.6 PRESENT EMPLOYMENT SITUATION IN INDIA

According to NSS data the growth of employment during the one and half decades between 1972-73 and 1987-88 is 2 per cent per annum. During this period rural employment has grown at the rate of 1.75 per cent per annum. All sectors have registered higher growth of employment of more than 3 per cent per annum, excepting agriculture, which employs more than 2/3rd of the total working population. In agriculture, employment rose only by 1.37 per cent per annum during this period. Mining, electricity and construction, which together have an employment share of 5 per cent, witnessed a higher rate of growth of employment, i.e. 5.47 per cent, 7.06 per cent and 7.23 per cent respectively. In transport sector, which engages 2.5 per cent of the total working population, employment rose at an annual rate of 4.7 per cent. However, in manufacturing (employment share of 16 per cent) and in services (also having employment share of 16 per cent), the employment growth during this period is 3.61 per cent and 3.55 per cent respectively.

When we analyse the growth of employment from macro perspective, we find a declining trend over this decade and half. From 2.28 per cent during 1972-73 and 1977-78, the rate decreased to 2.2 per cent between 1997-98 and 1982-83 and further reduced to 1.5 per cent during 1983-1988. In organised manufacturing industry, the rate of increase in employment has substantially declined from 2.48 per cent during 1973-1977 to 1.36 per cent during 1983-1987. The growth of employment in unorganised sector is relatively higher than the organised sector. What is disquieting is that casual labour has significantly increased than self employed and regular salaried wage labour. During this period casual wage labour increased from 23 per cent to 30 per cent while on the other hand self employment declined from 61 per cent to 56 per cent and the regular salaried workers stabilised at 13.5 per cent.

In India unorganised sector still dominates with 90 per cent share of total employment in manufacturing. The burden of employment for unorganised informal sector is growing for obvious low absorption capacity of the organised formal sector.

13.7 ECONOMICALLY ACTIVE POPULATION

Economically active population means, those who are able-bodied and are capable to work or those who are in the working age group. International Labour Organisation (ILO) defined economically active population based on the age-group of the people. Those who are in the age-group of 15 to 64 are normally considered as economically active. Percentage of the economically active population in a country is an indicator of strength of employable people. In India economically active population is 57.4 per cent of the total population. It is pertinent to mention that all economically active population may not be employed, hence, the term is different from 'working population'. 36.8 per cent of the total population in India is 'working population'.

13.7.1 Change of Occupational Pattern in India

Structural change in the economy can be measured in terms of change in relative shares of incomes of factors of production in the major sectors of the Indian economy. Central Statistical Organisation (CSO) presents such estimates under following five categories:

    (i) Compensation of employees;

    (ii) Interest;

    (iii) Rent;

    (iv) Profits and dividends and

    (v) Mixed income of self-employed.

In India wage-employment has substantially increased over the years, which is evident from increased income shares under the 'Compensation of employees' head and decreased income share under the 'Mixed income of self-employed' head over the decades.

Distribution of Net Domestic Product, at factor-cost, over the decades for the three sectors, shows that share of primary sector (agriculture and allied activities) declined while the share of Tertiary Sector (service) and Secondary Sector (manufacturing) increased over the decades. The increase in share of tertiary sector is more significant than the increase in share of secondary sector.

Such structural changes in the economy are instrumental in bringing structural change in occupational pattern.

Apart from the structural change in the economy, technological change also played a crucial role in bringing structural change in occupational pattern in India. Technology is an important element in the distribution of the labour force amongst industries and sectors of the economy. The decrease of employment in agriculture over the decades and the virtual constancy in the proportion of the labour force employed in manufacturing are attributable primarily to technological change.

Usually, technological changes induce change in occupational structure through:

    (i) Creation of new functions;

    (ii) Dilution of skills;

    (iii) Substitution of manpower for technology and finally

    (iv) Variation in the range of existing functions.

Again from economic point of view, technology brings changes in the labour market. It is widely believed, particularly by Marxist School of Thought, that with technology, production becomes increasingly capitalistic, which again leads to the emergence of swelling of wage earners. This for its far-reaching effect transforms labour as an item of competitive sale and purchase and labour units further become more and more specific. Interestingly this smoothened the path of development of occupational labour market.

All these factors together helped in emergence of new educated white–collar working class.

Since technology significantly induces change in production system, sectoral distribution of employment change is not considered as a better indicator to signify changes in occupational pattern. However, from latest census report, we find that while sectoral distribution of employment in agriculture over decades shows a decreasing trend and secondary sector shows a marginal increase, the tertiary or service sector indeed shows a significant increasing trend in percentage share of employment.

Distribution of different occupational categories over the decades shows, that professional, technical and related workers have increased over the decades. A significant rise in clerical and related workers and workers in unclassifiable jobs, also indicates a major change in pattern of occupational structure in India.

13.7.2 Technology Upgradation and Employment in India

During the post liberalisation era, macro level economic restructuring vis-a-vis unit level production restructuring is taking place, which inter alia, displace a large section of working population from employment. Macro level change in employment levels due to economic liberalisation has already been focused earlier. What is more important to mention here is that Indian industries are now required to restructure their production, introducing technology efficient system to make their product qualitatively better to compete with international manufacturers. This, therefore, necessitates Indian industry to undertake redeployment programme of their existing workers by giving them suitable training. Government of India to counter this burden of unemployment started National Renewal Fund (NRF). NRF will extend facilities making fund available for training and redeployment programmes or for giving effect to voluntary retirement, production restructuring, apart from displacement of labour forces, upon flexibilisation of labour, wages, working hours and even work allocation.

To make them globally competitive, Indian industries are required to upgrade their technology, which inter alia, will result in large scale displacement, as discussed earlier. In addition, technology introduction will also change the occupational pattern by changing job content of industrial employees. We have separately dealt with this issue.

Apart from change in occupational pattern, Indian industries are also likely to face wage flexibility (both in paid wages and non-paid wages). This trend is already evident as we now find wide wage disparity between organisations, even though they are operating in the same region and even also manufacturing the same items or providing the same services.

Flexible working hours (FWH) is also another important change at organisation level. Although FWH in the form of staggered duty hours is all along in vogue for certain categories of employment and industries (both for convenience and technical feasibility), customer-orientation is now forcing upon many organisations (more particularly those who render services) to adopt a more institutionalised approach to FWH.

The present state-of-art-technology is more flexible. To produce as per customers' requirements is now compelling the organisations to change their prevalent practice of producing only some specific varieties. Such is also trend in service organisations. Therefore, to accommodate growing variety of products and to make organisations more transparent, flexible manufacturing systems are now increasingly being adopted. This technology is also instrumental to influence the job content of workers and/or employees. Trade specific skill and even, if not in all cases, atleast in some cases industry-specific skills are now being diluted for commonness of technology. To achieve better functional efficiency, jobs are now being restructured and workers are being trained to man such restructured positions in organisations. In most of the organisations, horizontal expansion of jobs (job enlargement) is going on, making work allocation more flexible. Service organisations are also considering in principle to confer double designation to their workers to ensure more productive utilisation of human resources.

Now we will discuss the effects of the technology on the labour market flexibility and investigate the institutional factors which together are forcing upon development of employee leasing as an alternative to permanent employment.

13.8 EMPLOYEE LEASING

Employee leasing is an arrangement under which an employer transfers all workers or groups to a leasing company which then assigns the same employees back to their original employer. Under the leasing arrangement employees get employed by employee leasing company, though may be working with the same employer (who leased them), may do the same job, work under same environment with same pay packets. Under changed circumstances, however, employers do not necessarily transfer their paid employees to an employee leasing company to get them back subsequently under leasing arrangement, but do not retain any employee on the permanent pay roll at all and send their requisition for required employees to the employee leasing companies from time to time, depending upon their production programme.

In the USA and other industrially developed countries in the world, all manufacturing and service organisations, to extent possible, are trying to avoid retaining employees on permanent pay roll and to the extent possible running their operations, which are highly flexible, hiring employees from employee leasing companies. Such manufacturing and service organisations, during the lean phase of production, send the leased employees back to employee leasing company to gain relief from wage cost burden for the idle time and to achieve economic efficiency.

13.8.1 Employee Leasing In India

Employee leasing is not a much known concept in India. However, etymologically employee leasing is quite akin to an instiutionalised approach to Contract Labour System, which is prevalent in India and even legally sustainable.

The most formidable challenge before the Indian industries during the post liberalisation era is to withstand price competition both at home and from abroad. Wage cost and non-wage cost (NWLC) together form a considerable percentage of total cost for Indian industries, particularly those in organised sector. The increased burden of NWLC made it inevitable for industries to restrict number of workmen on permanent payroll. Moreover, since production plans and programmes are highly flexible for industries, industries from time to time are required to engage workers to share the increased workload. Simultaneously, industries are also required to pay for idle working hours and also required to bear the brunt of NWLC for such workers. Institutionalised contract labour system, i.e. employee leasing, therefore, offers economic benefits to industries, which inter alia, enable them to sustain competition by cost minimisation.

This is a part of technological revolution in Indian industries gradually giving rise to the capitalistic mode of production in line with other developed countries in the world. This has made skill factor in labour units more and more specific and transformed the labour in an item for sale and purchase in the competitive market. Moreover, because of technology, industrial occupations have rapidly changed from productive to supportive activities. This changed phenomenon is particularly evident from the 1981 census which shows swelling of professional, technical and related workers, clerical and related workers over the other occupations. This, therefore, vouch for structural change in occupational pattern. Economic rationality and technical feasibility, therefore, sustain employee leasing in India.

However, in India we find contractor labour system as an alernative to employees leasing practice going on since long. What is important here is to understand that their lies wide difference in the approach to employee leasing in India and in the developed countries, who have succeeded in institutionalising employee leasing. It is observed that many favourable infrastructural changes, both at government and at institution levels, have been initiated by these countries to effectuate employee leasing successfully. Adequate State supported social security measures, safety net, insurance and pension schemes etc. sustain employee leasing in these countries without much problem. Moreover, leased employees in these countries are getting higher paid wages than employees on permanent pay roll, as organisations hiring leased employees can substantially gain from NWLC and overhead cost of personnel department, even after paying wages at higher rate to leased employees. Rights of leased employees also remain protected as their retirement benefits are taken care of by the leasing companies, subscribing to government sponsored schemes.

In India, our experience shows contractors' labourers are getting less than the workers on permanent pay role. Contractors' labourers and/or leased employees are engaged by organisations not only to save NWLC but even to gain substantially on paid wage costs (by paying less to them). Organisations engage them at substantially reduced wage rate than their permanent employees. A large number of placement agencies are extending such services to the organisation, in veil, making readily available various categories of manpower, details of whom they maintain in their data bank. In most of the cases such employees even do not know their employment status and continue as temporary employees for years together, which deprive them from all retrial benefits. Working as temporary employee on an organisation's pay roll for certain period make them statutorily eligible to enjoy permanent employment status. To avoid such complication, organisations prefer to retain the services of such employees hiring them either from contractors or from placement agencies (who are in veil leasing companies).

Thus, it is evident that in India, employee leasing is a standing practice, which is continuing flouting all social and institutional norms. This practice is further gearing up under New Industrial Policy of the Government of India which necessitates production restructuring through technological change. Technology upgradation, therefore, will affect the traditional employment relation, making it more contractual than institutional in the coming years.

Institutional theory empowers management to subordinate employees as they are in lower hierarchy of management, contractual theory advocates that the employer-employee relationship stems from the contract of employment.

13.9 RURAL LABOUR IN INDIA

In India more than 219 million people are engaged in agricultural activities. Adding the non-agricultural employment in the rural areas, the percentage of employment in the rural sector is as high as 65.5 per cent of the total work force of the country.

The National Commission on Rural Labour submitted its report to the government in July, 1991. Economic Reforms Programme of the Government of India hardly gave any emphasis on the prospects for agricultural and rural labour. The major features of the rural labour scene in India may be enumerated as follows:

1. The rural force, whether in agriculture or in non-agriculture is growing at a faster rate than the population growth in rural areas. This is particularly for reasons of decline in the proportion of self-employed households in agriculture, which is primarily for reasons of continued sub-division of holdings. This renders self-employed labour force in rural areas redundant compelling them to join the ranks of wage labour. In non-agriculture, employment in rural areas (household industries) is declining under the impact of technologically efficient modern industries.

2. Substitution of capital for labour in agriculture is also responsible for decline in rural employment.

3. Slow rate of public investment in agriculture is also responsible for deceleration in employment of rural labour. Government level survey in 1991 indicates growth of employment in rural areas decelerated from 2.5 per cent per annum during the seventies to less than 1 per cent over the eighties.

4. Rural labourers in India have very little access to the minimum needs like education, health care, drinking water, fair price shops/public distribution system, social security benefits, etc. Thus living conditions of rural labour have not improved even though social economic development process improved the levels of living condition of a small section of working class, i.e. the urban workers in organised sector.

5. The economic reform process by reducing the farm subsidies is further affecting the rural employment as farm owners will henceforth be more interested to employ technology efficient systems to increase the agricultural output replacing agricultural workers.

6. There is an increasing trend to corporatise the agriculture under large industrial units both by employing technology efficient production system and by using improved variety of seeds. Such corporatisation process on one hand

resulted in taking over of small land holdings, replacing the workers engaged therein and on the other reduced the overall rural employment substituting capital for labour.

7. Another recent phenomena is to emphasise on the selection of crops. It is evident that most of the agricultural land is now embarking on production of commercial crops, which are used as inputs of industries. Long range reaping of benefit by shifting the cultivation from food crops to teak wood is also a major phenomenal change in Indian agriculture. Since such crops, i.e. commercial crops and teak wood relatively require less labour inputs (as they require more technology-efficient monitoring system), overall employment in the rural areas is significantly decreasing in the recent years.

The economic reform programmes of Government of India utterly ignored the importance of rural or agricultural employment which still enjoys a high percentage of total employment share in India. The National Commission on Rural Labour emphasised on the need for developing rural human resources, providing social security to the rural workers, provisioning employment guarantee and also strengthening public distribution of essential commodities, in line with the on-going economic reforms programme to improve the living standards of rural labour.

Very recently, government has instituted Employment Assurance Scheme (EAS) to ensure wage employment to the rural labour at least for 100 man-days during the lean agricultural season. To start with, the scheme has been implemented in 1700 backward blocks, primarily situated in drought prone desert, tribal and hill areas. A Revamped Public Distribution System (RPDS) is also in operation. Water and soil conservation, afforestation, agro-horticulture, silvipasture under watershed development and minor irrigation works are also on the priority agenda of the government. To promote equity, social justice and human resource development, it is, therefore, necessary to augment government sponsored activities in the rural areas as a part of the on-going economic reform process.

13.10 ABSENTEEISM

Absenteeism is a total man-shifts lost because of absences of the total number of man-shifts scheduled to work. It, therefore, signifies unauthorised, unexplained, avoidable and wilful absence from work. Normal absence is excluded from this category as an employee usually takes leave of absence with prior permission of the authority to meet his own personal exigencies. Such exigencies may be on the ground of sickness, certain domestic eventualities, accidents, etc. In all the cases, an employee may not take prior permission from his employer but may regularise his absence giving an intimation within a scheduled period of absence. In most of the cases, if an employee remains absent from work for more than 3 consecutive days without any intimation, it is considered as wilful or unauthorised absence. This, therefore, makes an employee liable to give intimation within 3 days from the date of his absence to regularise his leave. Absenteeism is, therefore, a wilful or habitual absence from work and not any other types of absence.

Wilful or habitual absence contributes to production loss and, therefore, it is a major problem for the management. The problem of absenteeism at macro level in India varies from industry to industry. Such rate normally varies from 7 per cent to 30 per cent. Also it varies from occupation to occupation. The worst affected industries for absenteeism are Mining, Textile, Jute, Plantation and Engineering.

Although there are a number of studies on problems of absenteeism at unit level, macro-level data on absenteeism in India is yet to be available to study the phenomenon both behaviourally and economically.

National Productivity Council carried out a survey to understand the magnitude of absenteeism and could find that personal sickness, family sickness, domestic and social exigencies are the most important factors for absenteeism in Indian industries. Other factors of absenteeism like drunkenness, poor inter-personal relationship, genuine transportation problems, need for leisure, etc. are responsible for relatively less percentage of absenteeism. Whatever may be the factors for absenteeism, any organisation needs to ensure better working environment, good inter-personal relationship, less industrial fatigue, adequate welfare facilities, motivation, quick redressal of grievances for reducing the rate of absenteeism. If all the above measures do not succeed, organisations need to educate workers and give counselling to make them aware of the effect of absenteeism, duly mentioning the financial loss sustained by them (in terms of wage-loss) and problems which the organisation suffer.

13.11 LABOUR TURNOVER

Labour Turnover is the rate of change in the working hands of a particular organisation during a given period. It, therefore, signifies the shifting of work force from one organisation to another and also the loss of manpower due to discharge, retirement, death, etc.

The rate of Labour turnover is expressed in terms of accession and separation rate. Accession is addition to the work force while separation is deletion from the work force, for any of the reasons mentioned above. Labour turnover is a serious problem for the industry because of the following reasons:

    (i) High cost of recruitment to effect replacement;

    (ii) High training cost;

    (iii) Loss of supervisory and managerial time;

    (iv) Slow rate of output of the new incumbents;

    (v) Damage to the plant and machinery;

    (vi) High rate of scrap and waste, etc.

In India due to less scope for job-mobility, labour turnover, job change or job switch is not a serious problem excepting in some particular occupations where knowledge and skill of workers are relatively more. In high profile jobs, turnover is more for obvious increased scope of job switch.

To encounter the problem of Labour turnover, it is necessary for the organisation to initiate same action as pointed out in the case of managing the problem of absenteeism earlier. However, little more attention is required to sustain employee motivation fulfilling both their intrinsic and extrinsic needs.

REVIEW QUESTIONS

1.   What are the factors that need to be considered for analysis of demand and supply for labour? Clearly explain those indicating their relative importance.

2. In what way labour market is different from other markets? In the context of the recent economic policy, explain the characteristics of Indian labour market.

3. Briefly point out the history of Trade Union Movement in India.

4. Do you think trade unions in India are becoming defunct institutions? Give adequate justification for your answer.

5. What are the challenges being faced by the Indian trade unions in recent years? Briefly discuss in the context of recent economic liberalisation programme of the Government of India.

6. In what way unemployment is related to Balance of Payment problems? What are your suggestions to solve such problems?

7. Briefly discuss Keynesian Income Generation Model in relation to unemployment and Balance of Payment deficit.

8. What are the different types of unemployment? In India what types of unemployment are more prevalent and why?

9. Briefly discuss the present employment situation in India in relation to current economic liberalisation programme of the Government of India.

10. Do you think that in India we are experiencing a change in the occupational pattern? Give justification for your answer.

11. In what way technology upgradation influences employment in India?

12. In what way Employee Leasing in India is relevant? Do you think that in India we can institutionalise this concept? Give justifications.

13. What are the problems of rural labour in India? What major roles the National Commission for Rural Labour has played to alleviate such problems?

14. Briefly discuss the problems of absenteeism in Indian industries.

15. Short Notes:

    a. Human Capital

    b. Internal Labour Market

    c. National Renewal Fund

    d. Voluntary Retirement Scheme

    e. Internal economic imbalance

    f. Technology Equilibrium

    g. Educated Unemployment

    h. Economically active population

    i. Labour Turnover

    j. Knowledge workers